...eap dpæn hæle... dern...
...and com þa to þecede pu...
...um bedæled dimu sona on apn pyr
...dum þæt syþðan he hipe þolmum
...man · on bpæd þabeilo hydig ða
...bolgen þæs þecedes mu þan raþe
æfter þon onfagne flor feond tred
node eode yrre mod him of eagum stod
ligge gelicost leoht unfæger seseah he
inþecede þinca manige sþefan sibbe
ge dpiht samod æt gædeie mago þin
ca heap þahis mod ahlog: mynte þæt
hege dælde ær þon dæg cpome · atol
aglæca anpa ge hpylces lif pið lice þa
him alum þer pæs pist pylle þenne þæs·
pid þagen þhe ma noste man na
cynnes dicgean oþer þa mihr hyd spyd
be heold mæg hige laces hu se man
scada under þær gripum ge faran pol
de nefþe aglæca yldan þohte

Kings Beasts and Heroes

THE MONSTER OF NOVES

Gwyn Jones

KINGS BEASTS and HEROES

London
OXFORD UNIVERSITY PRESS
New York   Toronto
1972

Oxford University Press

OXFORD LONDON NEW YORK
GLASGOW TORONTO MELBOURNE WELLINGTON
CAPE TOWN IBADAN NAIROBI DAR ES SALAAM LUSAKA ADDIS ABABA
DELHI BOMBAY CALCUTTA MADRAS KARACHI LAHORE DACCA
KUALA LUMPUR SINGAPORE HONG KONG TOKYO

ISBN 0 19 215181 9

Printed in Great Britain
by W & J Mackay Limited, Chatham

Contents

Illustrations

The three figures reproduced on pages xxvi, 62, and 120 are: a solid gold belt-buckle, 5.2 ins long and weighing 14⅝ oz, from the Sutton Hoo ship burial (British Museum); the bronze dog (a wolfhound?) from the Romano–British Temple of Nodens (Irish Nuada, Welsh Nudd) at Lydney, Glos. (in the possession of Lord Bledisloe); a mounted hero or huntsman or god from a Vendel helmet (after Montelius, *Kulturgeschichte Schwedens,* Leipzig, 1906).

The endpapers show two pages of the *Beowulf* manuscript, British Museum MS, Cotton Vitellius A.15, folios 148ʳ and 148ᵛ, reproduced from the Beowulf Facsimile, Early English Text Society No. 245, 2nd edition by Norman Davis, 1959 for 1958. The folios relate to Grendel's attack on the royal hall where the watchful Beowulf and his sleeping companions await him. The lines beginning Ða com of more on folio 148ʳ to the end of folio 148ᵛ are translated on page 13 below.

Acknowledgements

It is a great pleasure to me to record the kindness of those who have contributed to the making of my book. First there are the editors and scholars whose major contributions to medieval literary studies have eased and influenced my own ruminations. Many but not all of them are listed in the select bibliography or mentioned in my footnotes. Thereafter my thanks go most of all to my friend and colleague at Aberystwyth, Professor Thomas Jones, who has once again made me free of his learning both published and private, and has read almost half my manuscript. My friend and colleague at Cardiff, Professor A. O. H. Jarman, has with similar generosity subjected what I say about *Culhwch and Olwen* and the *Gododdin* to a close and helpful scrutiny. I owe thanks to Professor Kenneth Jackson of Edinburgh University for permission to quote four stanzas from his published translation of the *Gododdin*, and gladly acknowledge the stimulus of his Gregynog Lectures at Aberystwyth in 1961 on the international popular tale in a context of early Welsh literature. The passage from the *Bjarkarímur* is reproduced from G. N. Garmonsway, Jacqueline Simpson, and Hilda Ellis Davidson, *Beowulf and its Analogues*, by kind permission of the authors (I refer particularly to Miss Simpson, the translator) and the publisher, Messrs J. M. Dent and Sons. For Saxo Grammaticus I have quoted the classic translation of Oliver Elton (1894), and would willingly express an obligation to the (to me unknown) holder of copyright. On the few and fleeting occasions when, other than as translator, I have quoted from myself my thanks are due to Messrs J. M. Dent and Messrs E. P. Dutton of New York for some sentences from my Introduction to the Everyman Library edition of *The History of the Kings of Britain*, to the Oxford University Press, and to the *Times Literary Supplement* and its Editor.

I have listed in the appropriate context the libraries and museums, and other institutions or individuals to whom I owe my illustrations, and thank them both warmly and formally for permission to reproduce copyright material. I acknowledge with no less warmth courtesies shown me by Aktiebolaget Allhem Bokförlaget, Malmö; Hartmans Kortförlag A.B., Uppsala; Lord Bledisloe; Dr. D. Slay and Dr. M. Mills of the University College of Wales, Aberystwyth; Mr. W. O. Evans of the Department of English at Cardiff; Mr. Christopher Sandford; the Early English Text Society and its President, Professor Norman Davis; University College, Cardiff; and the Welsh Arts Council.

My deepest gratitude, as ever, is owed to my wife Alice, and it is to her that I inscribe my book.

University College   GWYN JONES
Cardiff

Introduction

THE AIM OF THIS BOOK IS TO EXAMINE THE SUBSTANCE and method, and more particularly the story-content and story-telling, of three justly famous works of medieval literature, one English, *Beowulf*, one Welsh, *Culhwch and Olwen* (*Culhwch ac Olwen*), and one Norse, *King Hrolf's Saga* (*Hrólfs Saga Kraka*). All three are narratives—by rough definition a verse epic, prose wondertale or romance, and legendary saga—and to all three their story is vital, for without it they would not exist. All three in respect of their narrative are heavily or even entirely dependent on earlier and for the most part identifiable story material. That is, they are not inventions or originals, but works of reproduction, re-arrangement, and re-creation. Every English listener knew that Beowulf would overcome Grendel and Grendel's Mother, and kill and be killed by the Dragon. Every Welsh listener knew that with the help of Arthur and his men Culhwch would achieve the Giant's tasks and win the Giant's Daughter. Every Norse listener knew that king Hrolf would save his life at Uppsala and lose it at Lejre, and all his Champions with him. This was no more to their or their story-tellers' disadvantage than it is for today's reader to know with Chaucer that Criseyde will betray Troilus, and with Stendhal that Napoleon will lose the battle of Waterloo. Inevitability is a more powerful instrument of the narrator's art than novelty or last-minute surprise, and the gratification of knowledgeable expectancy as much a challenge to the story-teller as it is pleasure to his audience.

The act of writing made it a literary challenge. All three works under discussion are written not oral compositions, though in the nature of the case produced by unknown authors for unidentified audiences in circumstances and for reasons to be surmised. Inevitably this almost complete absence of facts invites conjecture, and sometimes conjecture at more than one remove. Thus, when we speak of an 'author' we can have little more positive in mind than a conviction that works of art such as these are not normally produced by syndicates, copyists, editors, or redactors, but by men who give their work the impress of their personality and intention, together with a further conviction (which I confess to holding) that in respect of *Beowulf* absolutely, *Culhwch and Olwen* tantalizingly, and *King Hrolf's Saga* assuredly, one recognizes this impress and feels acquaintance with the thoughts, feelings, tastes, and abilities of an individual artist. Sometime, somewhere, somehow, somebody gave each of these works the character it still retains; and that somebody, though we possess neither his name nor the original of what he produced, is its author and a legitimate subject of literary speculation.

It is likewise legitimate to speculate how his work was communicated to an audience. *Beowulf* looks and sounds a highly organized performance addressed outwards from its author. It has the air of a formal public utterance meant to be heard, and heard more than once, by those whose interests and edification it catered for. Presumably the mode of communication for all save the comparative and fortunate few able to read it for themselves was by recitation or reading aloud in a suitable number of instalments. Today, still, on the printed page its manner is large and ample. It speaks like its own messenger bearing tidings of Beowulf's death (2897-9), *ofer ealle*, for the attention of all. *King Hrolf's Saga* is less exhortatory, more familiar, and more of a tale—a good yarn to tell and hear, in that something is happening to somebody all the time. Unlike *Beowulf* it is preserved in many manuscripts, late ones to be sure, but there is no reason to doubt that like other sagas it was copied for reading by those who could read and for reading aloud to those who could not. *Culhwch and Olwen* is more of a problem. The likeliest explanation of its composition (and likeliest does not necessarily mean likely) is that it was the deliberate attempt of a story-antiquarian to bring together a sequence of folktales which he associates with a number of folktale or legendary figures, but for what reason and audience we do not know. We can guess at a 'bookman's' exercise in story-salvage and restitution, but this only leaves us with another why. And for all three works we lack the reasonably assured dates which could make conjecture better based.

Even so, one consequence of a writer's setting quill to vellum is that he transfixes his version of the story material at a point in time.

The material may, of course, continue to enjoy a long and fruitful life in oral forms with or without regard to the written version; and there is the added complication of the time-lag between an author's act of composition and the date of the manuscript in which we find it preserved. All three works belong in terms of events and persons to the sixth century, in Denmark and Geatland (*Beowulf*), in Britain (*Culhwch and Olwen*), and in Denmark, Norway and Sweden (*King Hrolf's Saga*). They were composed, we believe, in the eighth century; between 1050 and 1100; and not long before the year 1400, respectively. They are preserved in manuscripts of *c.* 1000, *c.* 1300–25, and the second half of the seventeenth century. Their authors' sense of past time, their reading of the sixth century in particular, and their notions of concordance between past time and their own, are matters almost entirely obscured from us. But when all such barriers to knowledge have been recognized and allowed for, the fact remains that author and scribe between them provide us with a literary work, detached and observable, and this is the essential requirement of a literary investigation.

I hope my book will have interest for others besides readers of *Beowulf*, *Culhwch and Olwen*, and *King Hrolf's Saga*, for when assessing their narrative content and sources it necessarily attempts a series of soundings in what I believe is becoming an important and attractive area of literary study—the foundations and structure of medieval literary narrative. There is general agreement that the main story elements in that considerable body of writings of which these three are representative are myth, folktale, heroic legend, and history, though there is substantial disagreement both in general and particular as to which of them is which. It is in any case an over-simplified list of narrative categories, for what we in fact find ourselves confronted with is myth, folktale, heroic legend, legendary history, historical tradition, and history. These, we soon discern, have been laid under tribute in very different proportions. The use of myth (which at best means myth in decline) and of history (which at most means not immediately discountable factual statement) is hardly more than minimal. The true stuff of our three works belongs not with these, as is still often maintained, but in varying degree with heroic legend—that is, with hero-tale accredited to a known and named hero belonging in the early traditions of a tribe, people, country or race, and not to any anonymous folktale figure—together with the folktale (I should prefer to say wondertale) with which heroic legend is deeply involved and from which some of it has emerged, and to a lesser extent with the legendary history into which a good deal of heroic legend and wondertale has developed. Clearly these are statements which require amplification and if possible proof, and these I believe the body of my book will provide. In general I have sought to proceed by asking four questions about each work: 'What is it?' 'What is it about?' 'How is it done?' and 'How well is it done?' Perhaps questions one and two should have sufficed. The other two are there because it is not in human nature to identify, outline, and describe the story material of a work of literature and give no thought to how, and how well, an author has used it.

And now to define my terms. Not, I think, that it is possible to define them so sharply that every element of every story can be allotted to one precise and inviolable sphere. It is nowadays not too difficult to distinguish between myth at one edge of the spectrum and history at the other, and hardly more so to separate wondertale from historical tradition. The real task is to distinguish between myth and wondertale, myth and heroic legend, wondertale and heroic legend, heroic legend and legendary history. And this chiefly for two reasons. First, a good story never dies, but shows powers of persistence and renewal from one age to another. The principal themes of myth, wondertale, and heroic legend are at once too entertaining and in-structive, too adaptable to circumstance yet constant to the human condition, for them not to live on now in this guise now in that. Second, we do not have clear and accepted definitions of what these kinds are, so that we may all agree what it is we are trying to distinguish, and from what. This is especially true of myth. The seeker after truth in that delphic arena soon finds himself echoing M. Lévi-Strauss's heartfelt cry that studies in the field of mythology today as fifty years ago are 'a picture of chaos', and ruefully accepting Professor Kirk's corrective yet confirmatory addendum that there is 'no one definition of myth, no Platonic form of a myth against which all actual instances can be measured'. However, this is a literary not an anthropological essay, and a restricted one at that. I have therefore found it convenient to adopt Stith Thompson's declaredly minimum definition that 'myth has to do with the gods and their actions, with creation, and with the general nature of the universe and the earth.'[1]

[1] Claude Lévi-Strauss, 'The Structural Study of Myth', p. 82, in *Myth, A Symposium*, ed. Thomas A. Sebeok, Indiana University Press, Bloomington and London, 1968; G. S. Kirk, *Myth, Its Meaning and Functions in Ancient and Other*

This serves to distinguish myth from folktale and heroic legend in a plain if somewhat blunt way, and keeps me from judgements I am not competent to make in respect of ritual, etiology, origins, and content. A myth, let us say, will be concerned with phenomena such as these: divine or part-divine beings and their worship; the origins of things and creatures; times and seasons; powers and forces; ends and destructions; and by virtue of this concern will be categorically identifiable.

It follows that when a story displays no divine protagonist and reveals no cosmic significance I consider myself to be not dealing with myth, though quite possibly with myth becoming or already become something else—usually wondertale or heroic legend. When Thor, a god, fights with the Midgarth Snake, a cosmic monster which seeks the destruction of Midgarth, the World of Men, kills it, and in later versions of the story is likewise killed by it, that is myth. When Beowulf, a man, fights with, kills, and is killed by a dragon which would have troubled neither him nor his people had it not been robbed of its treasure, that is not myth but heroic legend evolved from wondertale. Whether this wondertale evolved from myth, or is otherwise related to it, is a proper subject of inquiry, and one which has been pressed hard in a context of vegetation-myth, nature-myth, post-pagan (i.e. Christian) myth, and most recently of all combat-myth. But one can recognize that *Beowulf* preserves husks of myth and reminiscence of mythological story and still see the poem as neither myth nor mythological story in any meaningful use of those terms. The *Beowulf* poet's business is with a non-divine hero of wondertale descent whom he associates closely, constantly, and prolongedly with the antecedents of northern tribal history and has fight to the death a destructive but conventional and non-apocalyptic foe. If this is allowed to be a fair working principle, then as we have said, and will in due course show, the use of myth in a pure and pristine form is minimal in *Beowulf* and even more patently so in our other two subjects of study. Fortunately, agreement on every detail or even area of interpretation is not essential to an approval of the main thesis. And emphatically it is no part of that thesis that the authors of *Beowulf*, *Culhwch and Olwen*, and *King Hrolf's Saga* made such distinction between myth and wondertale, wondertale and heroic legend,

---

Cultures, p. 7, Cambridge University Press, 1970; Stith Thompson, 'Myth and Folktales', p. 173, in *Myth, A Symposium*.

and the various striations of history as we, or would have thought it profitable or even possible to do so.

It may appear at this point that I have adopted a set chronology for myth, wondertale, and heroic legend, as though they were born into the world in that order—which is a thesis impossible to maintain. The literary expression of all three belongs rather late in time, and the evidence for precedence or succession is meagre and unsure. Whether, for example, the story of an unnamed man or named hero who fought with animal, fabled animal, monstrous beast or monster, existed, maybe widely, before it attained the dignity of myth, who shall say? That wondertale is the detritus of myth is an assumption, and that heroic legend is an exaltation of wondertale is another. Both sound reasonable, but they stand a long way off from proof. One of the chief persons of *Culhwch and Olwen* is Arthur; another naturally enough is Culhwch; and there are Arthur's men. By the time *Culhwch and Olwen* was written down these were already heroes in the exacting sense that they were known and named exemplars of the Heroic Age of Britain, hewers with steel and feeders of ravens, boars of onset and bulls of battle; but in *Culhwch and Olwen* they have been seized and held at folktale level as achievers of marvels, warlocks and wizards. Which Arthur came first—the Arthur of historical tradition or the Arthur of wondertale? And which Culhwch—the lion-like warrior of the Llywarch Hên poetry or the folktale winner of the giant's daughter? Certainly the Beowulf myth (or what has been regarded as such) was antecedent to *Beowulf* the heroic poem; and the heroic poem in its turn appears to draw much more from the patterns of wondertale associated with the Bear's Son and Aarne-Thompson's Type of the Folktale 301 than it subsequently contributes to them. One concludes that the chronological sequence of categories is not fully established, and where established is not immutable. Still, in respect of *Beowulf*, *Culhwch and Olwen*, and *King Hrolf's Saga* it appears certain that by the time poem, romance, and saga were composed, wondertale and heroic legend had taken over from such myths as may once have been relevant to them. For this reason I have put myth first of their categories of story material.

Which brings us to folktale, and more specifically to the kind of folktale which its most recent and distinguished classifiers call tales of magic, and I without originality call wondertale. Folktale is the agreed if unsatisfactory title for that almost endlessly diversified mass of popular story or fiction, often more than national in its dispersal, which has existed by word of mouth over many centuries or even millennia, and been recounted by thousands of story-tellers of different kind and quality in different countries or continents and before every kind of audience. Grave, comic, delicate, gross, rational, supernatural, religious or magical; informative, cautionary, didactic, lying, riddling, peasant-headed or romantic, it was as necessary to early narrative literature as grass to early agriculture. Our present three texts, as it happens, relate closely to those varieties of wondertale which treat of supernatural adversaries and helpers, but other texts, other proto-types, and too much significance should not be read into this partly fortuitous circumstance. No one theory has covered the origins of folktale, and no one explanation its diffusion, but clearly it met a basic and persistent human need—the need to tell and be told a story—and continued to do so when the written word began to take over from the spoken, the change of medium itself allowing the artist life-renewing variations on the famed familiar themes. Historians and poets, fabulists and homilists, the fashioners of romance and com-pilers of saga were among those who drew on its copious store, as *Mabinogion* and *Táin*, the *History of the Kings of Britain* and the *Lives of the Kings of Norway*, Saxo Grammaticus and *Gesta Romanorum*, Chrétien de Troyes and Chaucer himself bear witness. Popular story and inter-national wondertale helped shape not only the Oldest Animals and Unending Battle, the Sleeping Princess and Perilous Maiden in the European mind, but Alexander, Arthur, and Charlemagne too; and have charged and sustained the story-teller's imagination from Herodotus to the Ballads, the Apocrypha to the *Arabian Nights*, and from *Beowulf* in the older Old World to William Faulkner in the newest New. Folktale of this high and honourable definition was adult fare, welcome to the noblest and best, and co-extensive not with age, class, and occupation, but with the whole range of society.

I have already stressed in my second and third paragraphs our state of ignorance with regard to our three authors, their reasons for writing, and how these writings were communicated to their audi-ence. That might appear to fend off further discussion as more or less useless. Yet one important thing remains: to emphasize their ex-cellence. If these authors were alive today they might be busied in a publishing house, employed by the B.B.C., or fed and fostered by a University Department of English—but we should nonetheless describe them as professionals. That is to say, they were men who, whatever else they might be and do, had acquired the skills and tools of the author's trade by precept and example, and were self-aware and regardful in their employment. In a phrase, they knew their business; and in the words applied by the *Beowulf* poet to the king's thane who entertained his fellows as they rode back from Grendel's mere (871–902, see p. 31 below), each stands revealed as 'a man laden with eloquence, his mind charged with story, who remembered so many things of old.' By this I do not mean that our authors in person discharged their eloquence upon an audience attendant for the occasion. They may have done so, but we cannot say of any one of them that he had that kind of gift. Not every author had the talents ascribed to himself by Sturla Thordarson, who wrote splendid prose and exciting history and in addition could tell a wondrous tale so bravely as to win a queen's compliment and esteem, and recite a poem so handsomely that no less partial a judge than King Magnus of Norway would pronounce: 'It is my opinion that you recite better than the Pope' (*Sturlunga Saga*, II, 271). But without echoing the compliment we may emulate the esteem, and see our three authors for what they are, men laden with eloquence, their minds charged with story, skilled refashioners of prized material in accordance with the requirements of their audience and the demands of their art, both of these in important respects dissimilar from our own. A close attention to what their narratives consist of, how they were put together, and how enhanced, may well make us less dogmatic in our approach to medieval authorship generally, more understanding of its problems and appreciative of its solutions—in a word, more willing to trust to the author. Just as it allows us to see *Beowulf*, *Culhwch and Olwen*, and *King Hrolf's Saga* as purposeful literary artefacts in their own day as well as objects of critical curiosity in ours.

This conducts us back to my original statement of purpose. My concern, I have said, is not with the whole wide world of myth, wondertale, heroic legend, legendary history and the rest, but, more narrowly, with the use three authors have made of it for their particular literary ends. The *Beowulf* poet used, maybe at several removes, two well-known, widely-dispersed, and frequently-repeated wondertales as foundation and framework of an ambitious poem which is not versified folktale but epical, heroic, heroic-elegiac, or even, in a sense more real to him than to us, 'historical' in nature. The immensely accomplished author of *Culhwch and Olwen* used yet another wondertale as foundation and framework of a fantastic, heroical, irregular, folktale-motif-studded prose narrative which, unless we continue to call it wondertale, we must needs call romance—the first romance, incidentally, in European literature to tell of Arthur and his court. The author of *King Hrolf's Saga* follows a tardier line in that his titular hero king Hrolf takes a good while to arrive on the scene, and his secondary hero Bothvar Bjarki a good while longer. The folktale ascriptions can be made with confidence, and the most important of them, relating to Little Bear, son of Bear and She-Bear, most confidently of all; but *King Hrolf's Saga* (*Hrólfs Saga Kraka*) is a saga, and the nature of saga is to proceed by means of linked sections in a chronological and genealogical way, so that no one folktale could underlie it in its entirety. This is no disadvantage to saga, and none to an inquiry into the presence of folktale and folktale-motif in three highly developed and interestingly diversified medieval literary kinds: epic, romance, and saga.

The circumstance that all three are written works shows us the process of story-blending and story-transformation caught at a significant point of arrest. In them we observe how one kind of tale and telling can become something else: wondertale becoming heroic legend, heroic legend entering the realm of legendary history, and the attachment of floating story-material to a named hero in a known geographical setting—in the case of *Beowulf* and *King Hrolf's Saga* a hero, moreover, subject to the conventions of an hierarchical society, and discharging the tasks, duties, and obligations incumbent upon him as an embodiment of the ideals of an heroic age. By such process the wondertale, as it were, grows up, acquires morality and a social purpose. *Beowulf* indeed almost entirely transforms wondertale save for its story-telling directives, for the poet not only moves on the levels of heroic legend and legendary history, but incorporates into his poem a system of morality, religion, wisdom and good behaviour, clearly and repeatedly set forth. *King Hrolf's Saga* stays short on morality and religion throughout, but in its second half promulgates a code of conduct uncompromisingly and even stridently heroic. Conversely, an inability or refusal or plain lack of intention to make its protagonists more than the denizens of folktale, and the absence of a morality higher or more elaborate than the simplistic impulses to action of that genre, go far to explain the buoyantly heartless tone of *Culhwch and Olwen*. Between them the three works offer instructively varied permutations of basic story material with such other concomitants of meaningful literature as were compulsive upon their authors. And can there be anyone who doubts the marked superiority of all three as works of art to the prototypes from which they were in large measure assembled?

I still need to say something about my use of the terms legendary history, historical tradition, and history, and find it easiest to approach them in reverse order. In our present context I would confine the term history to our authors' use, for whatever purpose, of known events and authenticated persons—and put a severe interpretation upon the words 'known' and 'authenticated'. It follows that the only authenticated (one still hesitates to use the word indubitable) historical event referred to in *Beowulf* is king Hygelac's defeat and death on a raid into Frisia *c.* 521; that *Culhwch and Olwen* contains no verifiable history whatsoever; and that modern Scandinavian scholarship pronounces as bleakly on *King Hrolf's Saga*. Historical tradition, however, is a different matter. Such tradition need not be true in this detail or that, or conceivably in any detail at all, but offers a large view of past situations and events from which cautious deductions can be made. Thus *Beowulf* tells of warfare between Geats and Swedes, and *King Hrolf's Saga* of warfare between Swedes and Danes, and since everything we learn about Dark Age conditions in Scandinavia testifies to a heroic ethos and martial practice there, we can accept the historical tradition of both works for what it is, a reflection of reality. Similarly I think we can accept Hrothgar-Hroar, Hrothulf-Hrolf, and Eadgils-Athils as reflections of reality, though not as reality itself. Legendary history is at a still farther remove from actuality, and often does no more than associate a legendary event with a name discoverable in historical tradition. King Hrolf's treasure-seeking visit to Uppsala and his heroic death at Lejre are cases in point. There was most surely a famed and wealthy stronghold of the Swedes at Uppsala, and men of might and riches had lived and died at Lejre since the Stone Age. What more natural than that well-intentioned antiquaries and inventors of histories should associate the august but shadowy Hrolf with both? And what more natural than that no weighable evidence for the association can be found? What more natural too than that both events, the ride to Uppsala and the defence at Lejre, as we shall see in the appropriate context, are heavy with wondertale and rich in folktale motifs? Scyld Scefing and Hrothgar's Heorot in *Beowulf*, and Arthur's exploits in *Culhwch and Olwen*, stand even farther away from historical tradition, in that confusingly indeterminate world where wondertale merges with heroic legend and heroic legend rubs shoulders with legendary history. Indeed, *Culhwch and Olwen* not only contains no history and no historical tradition, but hardly a trace of legendary history, and surprisingly little heroic legend either. It is therefore a more consistent reworking of international popular tale in a local context than *King Hrolf's Saga*, when we consider that saga's elaborate mixture of heroic legend, legendary history, and historical tradition with folktale, and altogether more so than the complex, serious-minded, and civilized poem we call *Beowulf.*

By design I have held my book within fairly strict limits. *Beowulf, Culhwch and Olwen*, and *King Hrolf's Saga* are extraordinarily rich in story and richer still in sources, analogues, and the allied illustrative apparatus. Each one of them could easily be the subject of a book much larger than this. So to keep within measure I have almost entirely excluded what archaeology and iconography can bring to their elucidation. In respect of *Culhwch and Olwen* I have passed over the wealth of Irish heroic saga; and have been the more niggardly in discussing the relationship of *Beowulf* and *King Hrolf's Saga* to Danish, Geatish, and Swedish legendary history and genealogical transmission in that I have summarized the problems elsewhere. Similarly I have made no sustained incursus into Germanic and Celtic religion and mythology, and judged it wise to avoid the fashionable modern Christian exegesis of *Beowulf*, much of which impresses me as being most strikingly of a kind with our great-great-grandfathers' exposition of the Song of Songs which is Solomon's as Christ's love for the Church, with special reference to the spiritual significance of the female navel. I have held back from a general discussion of heroic poetry and romance, and fenced out a wilderness of animals and their lore—the most obvious outlaw in Bear's Son Country being Sweet-foot, Honeypaw, Beewolf, Old Grandsire himself, the Bear. Dragons, mound-dwellers, immemorial prisoners, heroic assemblages, beard-reapings, and decapitations are but half a dozen of a score of topics which I have not let tempt me from my narrow path. Even in the realm of wondertale I have been content to indicate, leaving documentation to the majestic, indispensable, and it must be admitted formidable volumes of Antti Aarne and Stith Thompson.

However, cheerfulness keeps breaking in, and maybe I have evaded my own rules in the paragraphs on Bothvar Bjarki's sword (pp. 161–2), the pages on the *Gododdin* (pp. 51–5), and the chapter on 'Hunters and Beasts' (pp. 102–19). My excuse for this last would be that the hunting of the boar Twrch Trwyth seemed deserving of amplification from outside *Culhwch and Olwen*, and that a digression in favour of

Moby Dick and *The Bear* will show that literature has not seen the last of wondertale, reshaped and renewed, which tells of Kings, Beasts, and Heroes, in such metamorphosis as fits the changing world of men.

I hope the reader finds the book's illustrations both useful and illuminating. For the most part they depict Germanic and Celtic artefacts such as weapons and ornaments, or are portrayals by early and unknown artists of men and creatures, motifs and events, comparable with those mentioned in our texts. They are not offered as illustrations of *Beowulf, Culhwch and Olwen,* and *King Hrolf's Saga* in the literal sense. Rather they are illustrative of the real and fictional worlds reflected in these works. Often they are so in a quite factual way, like the Vendel and Sutton Hoo material, the Snartemo sword-hilt, the Torslunda helmet-moulds, and the pages of the *Beowulf* and Saxo manuscripts. The dragon fight from the Hyllestad portal and the fight with monsters from the Tyldal chair, the confrontation of dog and beast from Caerleon and the handsomely moustached crowned and stylized visage on the Åker belt-buckle, the Temple of Nodens dog and the Neuvy-en-Sullias boar, while less 'factual' are entirely relevant to the domain of wondertale and hero-story. A third group of pictures is not factual at all, but in its unfactual dimension is hardly the worse for that. The Monster of Noves is not Grendel or Grendel's Mother, who between them ate Hondscio to his hands and feet and left Æschere's severed head on the mere-cliff; but he is monsterly enough even so, with a human arm protruding from his devouring mouth and two long-visaged severed Celtic heads poised with hideous precision betwixt his fore and hinder paws. 'When I looked among the teeth of Gandereb, dead men were hanging in his teeth.' The long-tunicked, long-sworded warrior of Eglwysilan comes from a Glamorgan churchyard, not an illuminated manuscript, but in *Mabinogion* style he could raise a shout to make men lose their hue and beasts in the fields lose the fruit of their wombs, then boast his name and fill a seat unquestioned among Arthur's folktale ménage. So with the Gundestrup cauldron. It has nothing to do with *Culhwch and Olwen,* and nothing to do with Wales, but its magic-laden, god-and-beast-haunted, host-processional, fiercely active and not always comprehensible panels are a rich Celtic backcloth against which to see the Oldest Animals, the Freeing of the Prisoner, and the Hunting of the Wondrous Boar.

Finally, *Beowulf, Culhwch ac Olwen,* and *Hrólfs Saga Kraka* are not just works which happen to chime with my themes and ambitions.

They are honoured entries in the literatures to which they belong and the languages in which they are written. It can do nothing but good for them to become better known to the general reader for whom those languages are a barrier. I have therefore at all times quoted from them in translation. I think I have heard all the arguments against this genial practice, and in this day and age find them unconvincing. The passages from *Beowulf* and other Old English poetry have been prepared for the occasion; those from *Culhwch and Olwen* are from the translation of the *Mabinogion* made by Professor Thomas Jones and myself for the Golden Cockerel Press, 1948, and thereafter published in Everyman's Library, to which my page numbers refer; those from *King Hrolf's Saga* are from my *Eirik the Red and other Icelandic Sagas*, World's Classics, Oxford University Press, 1961, reprint of 1966; and the quotation from *Sir Gawain and the Green Knight* is taken from my translation of the poem published by the Golden Cockerel Press in 1952. My obligations in respect of material quoted from other sources will be found with my list of acknowledgements.

I. BEOWULF

1. Hero with Monsters

T HE OLD ENGLISH POEM *BEOWULF* IS ONE OF THE MOST precious relics of the early literature of England, and justly prized for a number and variety of reasons. For a start it is unique, in that no other poem of its size and kind has survived either in Old English or in the other Germanic literary languages to which English is related. Had it somewhere in its manuscript history succumbed to those perils of age, neglect, and fire to which we know it has been exposed, we should be left to speculate whether in fact the poets of any branch of the Germanic people were capable of composing a long sustained poem on a theme drawn from the world of pre-Christian Germanic tradition. In the light of such phenomena as the Sigurd lays of the Poetic Edda, the Latin *Waltharius*, the upturned horn of story which is Saxo's Danish History, and the Christian witness of the Old English *Andreas*, we might assume that they were, yet always be uneasy in the assumption. So the manuscript in which *Beowulf* is preserved, British Museum, Cotton Vitellius A 15, is a primary document not only for the English, but for the Germans, the Scandinavians, and their descendants in the New World as in the Old, with its proof that their ancestors had mastered the art of prolonged verse narrative and attempted that elevated mode of poetry which for the moment we may be content to describe as epic.

Moreover, this is a poem with claims on our regard far beyond its power of manuscript survival. It is most easily described as a poem of an epical and heroic nature, and in respect of its incident and action provides a notable synthesis of Germanic heroic legend and international wondertale as this latter was viewed in a Germanic context. Some have read it as pagan myth, others as Christian allegory, while some consider that its story remembers myth though its poet did not. Though not a true history, it touches closely on the matter of history, the triumphs and tribulations of kings, the winning of wars and loss of a kingdom, and has been pressed into service as a 'Gesta Danorum, Sveorum, Gothorumque', for the first half of the sixth century. Structurally, to a modern eye, it is less than perfect; even so its story of a young hero is compelling, of an old hero moving. It offers a noble picture of an age, its assumptions and behaviour, its hierarchical bases, and the gold-decked splendour of its warrior class. It conducts its protagonist through diverse settings and episodes, by land and sea, at court and in battle, in contests with monsters and courtesies with his peers. And our poet has time for much more than adventures and monster-riddings. He was conscious, like other Anglo-Saxon poets, of the world's lack of duration. Life, he knows, is fleeting; all things are hastening to their end. Warrior and corslet crumble side by side, fair maiden moulders in her fair array; the steed that paws the stronghold yard, the falcon winging through the hall, must falter and fall; rust frets and earth devours the toil of giants and works of wondrous smiths. Also, he was deeply concerned with values: the bonds that prevented society flying apart, heroic conventions, the claims of piety, a warrior's worth and woman's excellence, the qualities of good kingship, the means to fame. In the aged Hrothgar's words to Beowulf, we like the poem's hero are bidden: 'Know what manly virtue is.' In short, *Beowulf* is a poem of multiple source and episode, which combines the attractions of a brave tale with high moral seriousness, and offers a reading of life and experience. And finally, it is by any standards a good, even a fine poem; and there have been many to think it a great one—less for its movement and action, or fable, than because they find it a statement about human life and values by an artist who—by virtue of his technical ability, his command of words and metre, his power to present narrative, argument, reflection, mood, and feeling in verse—has given lasting significance to the thing he wrote, which is now the thing we read. Which means that *Beowulf* is worthy of our esteem for the reasons, no more, no less, for which we esteem all fine poetry.

We have by implication described *Beowulf* as a long sustained poem. To be precise, its length is 3,182 lines of Old English alliterative verse. There is so marked a break before line 2,200 that some scholars have thought that the concluding 983 lines, with their account of the Geat-Swedish wars, Beowulf's fight with a dragon, his death and funeral obsequies, were not part of the poet's original design, and either grew out of his ruminations during the writing of what we will call Part One, to which some such descriptive sub-title as 'Beowulf's Youthful Exploits' or 'Young Beowulf in Denmark' is commonly applied, or were added to Part One by a different poet. The first idea is possible but unprovable; the second appears altogether unlikely. Since we know nothing of the author as a person, and next to nothing of him as an author, and since we stand in ignorance of when and where and how and in what circumstance he composed his poem, we are of necessity confined to conjecture in respect of the poem's structure, and in modesty bound to admit that even the best conjecture may be wide of the mark. What we do know is that *Beowulf* is preserved in a manuscript copied about the year 1000, and that from what we know of the history of Old English alliterative verse it could hardly have been composed before the very late seventh century. The likeliest speculations have been in favour of the age of Bede (*c.* 680–730) in Northumbria; the reign of king Offa (757–96) in Mercia; and—since the discovery in the Sutton Hoo ship burial or cenotaph in East Anglia of a rich range of Vendel-style artefacts, helmet, sword, standard, shield, gold ornaments, all strongly reminiscent of artefacts described in *Beowulf*—the reign of an East Anglian king in the late seventh or early eighth century. There is no way of settling between these three claims, and we are left to conclude that some time in or near the eighth century an unknown person to whom for convenience sake we accord the title of 'author', composed, or put together, or in some way set his seal on the poem we call *Beowulf*, and that this poem was to all intents and purposes the one copied down in Cotton Vitellius A 15, alongside three pieces of Old English prose and a fragment of the poem known as *Judith*. Essentially, that is, we are considering the one and only surviving manscript version of *Beowulf*, and this because no other course makes sense.[1]

If this by formal definition is what *Beowulf* is, we may now ask ourselves, What is it about? Or if that is a question which invites a too complex answer just now let us replace it with, What story does it tell? In essence, the following.

A young man in the kingdom of the Geats, Beowulf by name, learns that a famed but ageing king of the Danes, whose name is Hrothgar, is denied the use of his royal hall Heorot by a monstrous creature called Grendel. He goes to Heorot with some companions, and fatally injures Grendel when he next attacks the hall by night.

The following night the hall is attacked by a second monster, Grendel's Mother, while Beowulf is sleeping elsewhere. He pursues her to her lair, which is at the bottom of a mere, kills her, and cuts off the head of the first monster, whom he finds lying there dead. He receives a rich reward from Hrothgar, and returns to his own home in triumph.

In later days, when Beowulf has become king of the Geats and ruled them well for fifty years, their land is ravaged by a dragon. Beowulf kills this dragon with the help of a companion, but dies of his injuries.

The immediate virtue of a summary as spare and undeviating as this is that it shows how Beowulf's first two exploits are linked together, while the third is removed in time, place, and also in kind. The first two are found in lines 1–2199, the third in lines 2200–3182. For convenience sake we will identify them by the titles (unknown to the scribe) of 'Young Beowulf in Denmark' and 'Beowulf's Fight with the Dragon'.

---

[1] (*a*) 'With all this, however, the poem continues to possess at least an apparent and external unity. It is an extant book, whatever the history of its composition may have been; the book of the adventures of Beowulf, written out by two scribes in the tenth century; an epic poem, with a prologue at the beginning, and a judgement pronounced on the life of the hero at the end; a single book, considered as such by its transcribers and making a claim to be so considered' (W. P. Ker, *Epic and Romance*, p. 158).

(*b*) 'I deal with the structure of the poem as it stands in MS. Vitellius A. xv, copied round about the year 1000, assuming that its text represents approximately the form given to the story by one man—original poet, or poet-editor, or accomplished reciter able to adapt and vary existing stories in verse' (K. Sisam, *The Structure of Beowulf*, p. 2).

I. SIXTH-CENTURY SWORDHILT WITH DECORATIVE PLATES
From Snartemo

As we have indicated, and will show in more detail later on, the basic story of Part One is enlarged, dignified, diversified, and often obscured by other story-material. For example, there is a pseudo-historical or, if the adjective is preferred, legendary preamble about the royal house of the Danes and the mysterious origin of the Scyldings. There is also a small amount of firm historical information about the Geats, their kings, and their warrings. There are several elaborately retailed scenes at the Danish court, in one of which Beowulf is verbally assailed by an enigmatic courtier named Unferth, and defends himself with a 'gab' or *gilp* about his skill and endurance as a swimmer and killer of sea-beasts, and in another of which the feasters in hall are regaled with the disaster-laden story of Finn the Frisian, Hnaef the Half-Dane, and the lady Hildeburh, wife of the one, sister of the other, and destined to forfeit them both, and her sons along with them. Elsewhere a minstrel tells of Sigemund son of Waels, Sigmund the Volsung, how he killed a dragon, so that he won fame and treasure, and of Heremod, a king among the Danes, how he was a burden to his people, so that they drove him away. There is a fairly determined retelling, in the guise of a foretelling, of the story of the Heathobard prince Ingeld's ill-fated marriage to Hrothgar's daughter Freawaru, and an interpolation even more intrusive when the poet elusively and puzzlingly tells of the vindictiveness of the lady Thryth (Modthrytho) and how she grew kinder after her marriage to king Offa. There is an old man's homily on the dangers of excessive pride addressed by Hrothgar to Beowulf, and warnings aplenty against faithlessness, impiety, cowardice, and greed. We are freely advised of the world's mutability and the transitoriness of all created things. But despite the interest and importance of all these matters, the basic story of *Beowulf*, Part One, is that set out above; and since Panzer's decisively documented but not overwarmly welcomed *Studien zum germanischen Sagengeschichte: I. Beowulf* appeared in 1910, we have been aware that its origins lie not in early Germanic heroic tradition, and certainly not in nature myths, but in the world of wondertale or popular story. And since the publication of Antti Aarne and Stith Thompson's *The Types of the Folktale*, 1928 and 1961, and Stith Thompson's *Motif-Index of Folk-Literature*, 1932–6

2. HEROIC AGE PORTRAIT WITH BOARS BELOW AND BIRDS OF PREY ABOVE
From Åker

and 1955–8, we know from which airt and region of that world.

The essential primitive story-material of the first part of *Beowulf* is that comprised in the folktale-type listed by Aarne and Thompson as 'The Three Stolen Princesses'. The apparent unlikeliness of the connection in the light of the title alone is a tax we must pay on the two scholars' immense and beneficial ordering of what had earlier been seen as an almost ungraspable mass of oral and written popular story. Unfortunately for the student of *Beowulf* their essay in scientific classification led them to abandon the title 'The Bear's Son' (under which earlier scholars including Panzer and Chambers had grouped the cognate folktale material), so that in *The Types of the Folktale* the Bear's Son motifs must be sought under the main head of 'The Three Stolen Princesses', Type 301, and to a considerably lesser extent under 'Strong John', Type 650A. There are interesting resemblances between the opening sections of these two, but unless in combination with the somewhat similar 301A (see A–T pp. 92–3) 'Strong John' does not include the hero's pursuit of a monster underground, his adventures there, and the circumstances attendant on his return to the upper world. That 'The Three Stolen Princesses' is an elaborate and complicated type of folktale, incorporating a great many motifs and episodes, and tolerating a considerable choice of alternatives by the story-teller without losing its story line, is immediately apparent when we read not only the analysis printed in *The Types of the Folktale* (2nd revision, Helsinki, 1961), but the motif-analysis supplied by Stith Thompson so as to display the 'anatomy of the tale'. These are transcribed in full so that what is taken over from story and motifs and what is omitted may be seen in perspective and proportion.

THE THREE STOLEN PRINCESSES.

I. *The Hero is of supernatural origin and strength: (a) son of a bear who has stolen his mother;* (b) of a dwarf or robber from whom the boy rescues himself and his mother; (c) the son of a man and a she-bear or [d] cow; or (e) engendered by the eating of fruit, (f) by the wind or (g) from a burning piece of wood. *(h) He grows supernaturally strong and is unruly.*

II. *The Descent. (a) With two extraordinary companions (b) he comes to a house in the woods,* or (b¹) *a bridge; the monster who owns it punishes the companions but is defeated by the hero,* (c) who is let down through a well into a lower world.—Alternative beginning of the tale: (*d*) *The third prince, where his elder brothers have failed,* (*e*) *overcomes at night the monster who steals from the king's apple-tree, and* (*f*) *follows him through a hole into the lower world.*

III. *Stolen Maidens.* (a) Three princesses are stolen by a monster. (b) The hero goes to rescue them.

IV. *Rescue.* (a) In the lower world, with a sword which he finds there, he ‖ lens. (b) The maidens ‖ olen.

‖ *v by his treacherous com-* ‖ he help of (b) a spirit ‖ r or (c) a bird, (d) to ‖ ed up.

‖ cesses when he arrives ‖ (c) sends his dogs to ‖ rings, (e) clothing, or ‖ impostors and marries

‖ Thompson, *Motif-Index of* ‖ n, Indiana, 1955–8. The ‖ supplied by the present

‖). *Remarkably strong man.* ‖ B635.1. *The Bear's Son.* ‖ *characteristics.* F611.1.1. ‖ 611.1.2. Strong man son ‖ n and she-bear. F611.1.6. ‖ ro engendered by eating ‖ . F611.1.10. Strong hero ‖ ero suckled by animal.

‖ *with extraordinary powers* ‖ *in woods.* G475.2. *Ogre* ‖ *stating monster. Youngest* ‖ . *Hero shoots monster (or animal) and follows it into lower world.* N773. *Adventure from following animal to cave (lower world).* F92. *Pit entrance to lower world. Entrance through pit, hole, spring or cavern.* F96. *Rope to lower world.* F80. *Journey to lower world.*

III. R11.1. Princess (maiden) abducted by monster (ogre). H1385.1. Quest for stolen princess.

IV. R111.2.1. Princess(es) rescued from lower world. *F601.3. Extraordinary companions betray hero.* K1935. Impostors steal rescued princess.

However, in thus digging for the deepest roots of Beowulf's story it is important not to fall into ancient error or new superstition. Demonstrably *Beowulf* is *not* 'The Three Stolen Princesses' retold in Old English verse. There are no stolen princesses, as in section III, so none can be rescued and wed; much of section V and practically all of section VI is consequently missing; and in section II we must manage without an apple-tree. This need not discomfit us: our concern is with those elements of the story which entered *Beowulf*, not those that fell by the story-teller's wayside. More than 600 versions or variants of 'The Three Stolen Princesses' have been recorded, a small proportion of them as void of princesses as *Beowulf*, and others where it is not the king's apple-tree but his palace which is prey to a monster who is injured and pursued by the hero. 'The Three Stolen Princesses' is itself an enormously variable complex of story-telling, and in addition it is far from being the complete story material of our poem. If then we now attempt a further summary of the first part of *Beowulf*, it is not in order to restore the rightly discarded view of earlier critics that the poem is a 'wild folktale' (which emphatically it is not), but to show how much of its subject matter, and how much of what is distinctive in the story it tells, must be related to a well-known, widespread, and many times reshaped and retold popular wondertale, and that unless we allow for this we shall not always know why our poet is doing what he is, nor fairly assess how well he is doing it. With an eye to the Aarne-

V. *K1931.2. Impostors abandon hero in lower world.* K677. Hero tests the rope on which he is to be pulled to upper world. K963. Rope cut and victim dropped. K1932. Impostors claim reward (prize) earned by hero. K1933. Impostor forces oath of secrecy. D2135.2. Magic air journey from biting ear. B542.1.1. Eagle carries men to safety. *F101.3. Return from lower world on eagle.* B322.1. Hero feeds own flesh to helpful animal. The hero is carried on the back of an eagle who demands food. The hero finally feeds part of his own flesh.

VI. K1816.0.3.1. Hero in menial disguise at heroine's wedding. T68.1. Princess offered as prize to rescuer. T161. Year's respite from unwelcome marriage. N681. Husband (lover) arrives home just as wife (mistress) is to marry another. H151.2. Attention drawn by helpful animal's theft of food from wedding table; recognition follows. H83. Rescue tokens. *Proof that hero has succeeded in rescue. H80. Identification by tokens.* H94. Identification by ring. H111. Identification by garment H113. Identification by handkerchief. Q262. Impostor punished. L161. Lowly hero marries princess.

Thompson analysis of 'The Three Stolen Princesses', we may now expand our earlier summary of Part One thus:

A hero of noble origin and superhuman strength, with the name of a bear (if, as appears likely, Beowulf = *Bēo-wulf*, the Wolf or Foe of Bees, i.e. the Bear), the attributes of a bear, and the troublesome boyhood typical of the Bear's Son, goes with his companions to cleanse a king's hall which is under night-attack by a monster. The monster kills one of the hero's companions, but the hero fatally injures him by tearing off his arm. In the morning a band of warriors follow his bloody tracks to a mere whose waters they see are stained with his life's blood. They return home rejoicing.

That night, while the hero is sleeping elsewhere, a second monster attacks the hall, and a second time a companion is slain. With a number of companions the hero pursues the new monster's tracks to a mere whose waters are stained with blood, and in an underground hall, with a sword which he finds there, he overcomes a she-monster and cuts off the head of the male monster he had fatally injured before. Some of his companions do not wait for his return; without good reason they leave the scene; but he gets safely up again with a precious swordhilt and the male monster's severed head. He receives his promised reward and returns to his own home in triumph.

But a tale's strength is in its telling, and its success registers not by summary but in the heart of a hearer. At this point we need to know something of how well and by what means the *Beowulf* poet has managed his story so far.

The poem's opening is formal and stately. We shall not meet our hero for a while, and even our first monster must stand expectant in the wings. For the beginning of the poem is antecedent to the beginning of its story. We have a prologue to traverse, whose concern is with Scyld, the legendary founder of the Danish Scylding (that is, Skjöldung) dynasty, who came from over the water a helpless child, to wax and thrive and cheer a troubled people, and at his life's end returned to the unknown source of his being. The relevance of this prologue to the rest of the poem has been contested: some see in its account of the funeral of an aged and beloved king a sad and distanced foreshowing of the funeral of another aged and beloved king at the poem's end; but this assumes a long memory, and most readers, one imagines, enjoy it separately and for its own sake, as a notable set-piece in the epic tradition, lofty in tone, elegiac in quality, and burthened with its proper mystery.

Then Scyld departed at the appointed hour, a great and mighty prince, to fare into the Lord's keeping. His beloved comrades carried him to the seaflood, as he had himself requested when the Scyldings' friend still ruled with his word. A well-loved leader of his country, he had held power for a long time. A ship waited there at the landing-place, icy and eager to be away, the king's own vessel, and they laid down their treasure-giver in her bosom, their glorious lord by the mast. There was many a treasure there, ornaments fetched from afar. I have never heard of a ship more handsomely decked with weapons of war and armour, swords and corslets. A multitude of precious things lay on his breast, which must make a far journey with him into the sea's dominion. For indeed they did not furnish him with lesser gifts and national treasures than those others did who sent him forth in the beginning over the sea alone, when he was still a child. Further, they set a golden standard high above his head, let the sea take him, gave him to the ocean. Their hearts were sad within them, their minds laden with grief. None can tell for sure, counsellors in hall or heroes under heaven, who received that freight (26–52).

If Prologue there must be (and ours is the first age of readers to be dubious of such courtesies) this can hardly be bettered; and once it is over we soon reach the three requisites of the basic wondertale of the first part of *Beowulf*: a royal hall, a monster who plagues it, and a hero who arrives to cleanse it. It was a hall built for magnificence and joy, the bestowal of gifts and drinking of wine, the sound of the harp and the minstrel's clear song. The monster was a creature of darkness, exiled from happiness and accursed of God, the destroyer and devourer of our human kind. Like the Norse *draugr* or animated corpse, he is in human form but devoid of humanity, though his size, shape, appearance, are what we make of them. Some *draugar* have a horrible smell, are rough-coated, or catlike, prodigal of blood and vomit; but of Grendel we are informed only that a horrid light most like to flame shone from his eyes, that it would require four strong men to carry his severed head, that the fingers of his torn-off arm were shod with long nails hard as steel—and that steel would not bite on him. When he first raids Hrothgar's hall, the antlered Heorot (Hart), he kills or carries off thirty fighting-men and eats them in his lair. Later we are told how he carried a glove or pouch at his belt to hold the victims. The hero who destroys him is a gallant young prince from far off, with thirty men's strength in his handgrip, and furbished in mind as in body for the task he undertakes. His very chivalry and pride, excessive as Byrhtnoth's at Maldon, serve their wondertale purpose, for he dispenses with sword and shield against an enemy who bears neither, and engages with him on his own terms, hand to hand—the only terms, as it happens, on which success may be won.

Then came Grendel stalking off the moor under the misty hill-slopes; he bore God's anger. . . . He came on under the clouds until he clearly recognized the wine-chamber, the gold-hall of men, shining with beaten gold. . . . The warlike creature, bereft of joy, came journeying to the hall. Though secured with forged bands the door sprang wide on the instant, as soon as he touched it with his hands. With havoc in mind, all swollen with rage, he dashed open the hall-entrance.

Swiftly then the fiend stepped on to the coloured floor, moved forward in anger. A horrid light shone from his eyes, most like to fire. Inside the hall he saw many warriors, a band of kinsmen sleeping all together, a brotherhood of fighting-men. His heart laughed within him; the loathsome creature planned before day came to part each one of them life from limb, now that he could hope to eat his fill.

But it was no longer his fate that he should devour more of mankind after that night. Hygelac's mighty kinsman was watching how this foul adversary would set about his brusque assault. The monster had no mind to delay, but promptly seized one sleeping man for a start, tore him unhindered, bit into his flesh, drank blood from his veins, swallowed him mouthful by mouthful, and had soon devoured the entire corpse, feet, hands, and all. He advanced still nearer, reached with his hands for the brave-hearted man where he lay, the fiend stretched out his claws towards him. Beowulf gave him a brisk and hostile welcome, propped himself on his arm. That pastmaster of wickedness soon realized that never in all this world, in any corner of earth, had he met with a stronger grip from any other man. He felt fear in head and heart, but might escape none the sooner for that. He longed to be gone, make tracks for his hiding-place, seek the noisy swarming-place of devils. His situation here was something he had never met with before in all the days of his life. And now Hygelac's brave kinsman remembered his evening's talk; he drew himself upright, and embraced him hard. His fingers burst: the giant was striving to get out, the hero pressed forward. If only he might, the infamous creature wanted to get farther into the open and flee to his fen-refuge. He knew that the power of his fingers was in the grip of a fierce foeman. It was a sorry journey that pernicious foe made to Heorot . . .

. . . A din arose, and was ever renewed. Terrible fear filled the North-Danes, every man of them that heard the wailing from the wall, God's adversary yelling his frightful lay, his song void of victory, hell's captive lamenting his hurt. He had him firmly in hand who was strongest in might of all men in that day and age. . . . His parting from life in this world and time was to be wretched; the alien spirit must travel a far way into the power of fiends. For now God's adversary, who before with joyful heart wrought so much violence on mankind, discovered that his bodily frame could not help him, but that Hygelac's brave thane had him in hand. So long as life was in him each was hateful to the other. The horrid creature suffered a hurt in his body; a widening wound grew visible at his shoulder; the sinews sprang apart, the tendons burst. Glory in battle was ordained for Beowulf. Grendel, hurt to death, must take flight away from there into the fen-refuges, seek his joyless dwelling. He knew only too well that he had reached the end of his life, his count of days (710–823).

The poet shows the same intense and steady purpose in his tale of Grendel's Mother, when after the joy and feasting that celebrated her son's death she arrived at Heorot, rescued the bloody trophy of Beowulf's success, killed a retainer where he lay sleeping, and left his severed head on the sea-cliff near her underwater home. Much care is given both to the scene and fashion of Beowulf's second exploit: the stony approach with its tall crags and narrow paths; the gloomy mere described in advance by king Hrothgar (see p. 57 below); the water burdened with sea-dragons and the shore from which beasts and monsters plunged sullenly away from the war-horn's challenge. Likewise Beowulf's preparations: his woven mail-shirt, shining helm and glittering sword; his lordly speech commending his men and treasure to Hrothgar's care, his warblade to its owner should death be his lot; his vow to win fame or perish in pursuit of it. Then, his preparations made and farewells taken, he dives down through the water for a long while of day. As soon as he reaches the bottom he is grappled with by its repulsive tenant. She fails to hurt his body with her sharp fingers, as do the sea-monsters with their tusks as she drags him to her dwelling. There, free from the flood as in a water-spider's bubble, he finds that his sword, brave blade that it is, will not bite on her; they wrestle and he flings her to the ground, but her strength is too great, he takes a fall, she throws herself upon him and seeks his vitals with her stabbing knife. In vain—God and his corslet protect him, he gets back on his feet, and sees then 'amid the armour a blade blessed with victory, an old sword made by etins, doughty of edge, the glory of warriors; it was the choicest of weapons, save that it was bigger than any other man could carry into battle, good and splendid, the work of giants.' With this he struck her so fiercely on the neck that her bones broke and the huge blade sheared through her body. A light shone forth, and by it he saw where Grendel lay dead, so struck off his head.

Meanwhile the Danes on the cliff above, observing the waters stained with blood, despaired of his life and rode sorrowfully for home. The Geats, sick at heart, stayed on, expectant of woe. Far below Beowulf observed a great marvel. The swordblade with which he had destroyed his foes began to melt away 'in battle icicles', long drips of gore, till only the ornamented hilt was left. It was with this and Grendel's head that he swam back up to daylight and met his rejoicing comrades.

The wondertale central to the first part of *Beowulf*, we have said, is that of the hero who rids the king's hall of the monster that plagues it, pursues it into some kind of lower world, and there is involved with another monster or monsters. The wondertale central to the second part of *Beowulf* is that of the dragon-killer. For the bases of Part Two, 'Beowulf's Fight with the Dragon', no extensive documentation is necessary. That a man fights a dragon is a commonplace of story, and appears in medieval literature as myth, folktale, heroic legend, saint's life, onomastic anecdote, romance, and quasi-history. So many heroes over so many centuries killed so many dragons, from Frotho and Fridlevus to Ragnarr Hairybreeks, and from Sigurd to St George, that the presence of one, or even two, dragons in a poem inclined to monsters excites no surprise. In general the dragon of north Germanic story is a creature of such ill presage, so steeped in evil, hell-bent on mayhem, and deeply in-volved with a treasure of gold, that on any one of these counts, much less all three, it must prove an adversary worthy of Sigemund early in the poem and of Beowulf nearer its close. It was a boast of king Volsung as of Hrolf Kraki, of Bothvar Bjarki as of Starkad the Old, that they never fled from fire or iron, and the flaming spew of a fire-drake was fire at its most legendary and horrendous. Our poet might have found a fitter and more consummatory foe for Beowulf's last adventure, because more famous, baleful, or legend-fraught, but it is hard to think of one. Bear, boar, *draugr*, a Swedish dreng or Frankish kemper, would all appear less primal and less awful. A man is a man, and a beast is a beast, but a dragon is a dragon is a dragon.

Is, not necessarily *was*. A number of scholars are coming to believe that Beowulf's three folktale exploits are in their nature closely connected: not two plus one, but an integrated three, either bound together by their not infrequent attribution to this or that member of a monster-slaying family; or by the recurrence in northern sources of apparent trinities of man-monster, woman-monster, and dragon-monster in human or animal shape; or by the identification of dragon with *draugr* (plural *draugar*, the animated dead), so that Beowulf's fight with the dragon is merely a variant on his fight with that other *draugr* Grendel and his Mother.[1] Some of this could be true, and more of it can be argued at length, with

---

[1] J. Fontenrose, *Python, A Study of Delphic Myth and its Origins*, California, 1959, Appendix 5, 'The Combat in Germanic Myth and Legend', pp. 524–34, sees Grendel as 'the Thanatos of German pagans' and his Mother as 'the old Chaos-Hag almost intact'. He considers the second part of the poem to be in large measure a parallel of the first.

'The dragon need not detain us as long as Grendel did; for the tale runs parallel in many respects. Beowulf is now an aged man who dies in the moment of victory, protecting his own Geatish land this time against the

analogues, parallels, and a little pleading to help. That a number of Norse stories reveal affinities and relationships between *draugr*, dragon, and a woman-troll is demonstrable, and as more and more stories are read with this in mind the demonstration will strengthen. Equally there is no doubt that Beowulf's closest parallels in Germanic wondertale fought with adversaries showing a family likeness to

---

destroyer. The *Beowulf* poet's purpose resembles that of the *Gilgamesh* poet: the mightiest hero cannot finally conquer death, but must in the end succumb to destiny. But the poet's creation belongs to literature; the tale that he used belongs to myth. Wiglaf, Beowulf's kinsman, the last of his house, who stood beside the hero in this combat, was truly victor in the fray; for he plunged his sword into the dragon's soft underbelly, delivering a mortal wound; then Beowulf, now near death from a poisoned wound, drew his knife and cut the monster in two. Beowulf, dying, gave his armor to Wiglaf as to a son; for he had no sons of his own. Therefore I place this combat under subtype II, wherein it is the slain god's son who fights and kills the monster.

'The dragon coincides fairly closely with the Grendel pair, and his tale with theirs, in the following respects. (1) He raided at night, spreading death and devastation far and wide among the Geats, and had to get back to his lair before dawn. (2) He lived in a dark cavern underground, beneath a burial mound on a rocky promontory beside the sea. (3) There he guarded an immense treasure. (4) He was huge of size, fifty feet long, and (5) he breathed forth blasts of flame. (6) Beowulf went to the barrow's rocky mouth to meet Firedrake, as we shall henceforth call him. (7) His companions fled, all except Wiglaf; much as years before his comrades at the mere's edge thought him dead and went back to Heorot. (8) Firedrake was fought and killed, and (9) his body was cut into two parts and cast into the sea. (10) The victor Wiglaf wielded a marvellous sword that giants had forged. Recalling the preceding discussion we can see some correspondence also in that (11) the victor succeeded to the throne, and (12) the Geats mourned the dead Beowulf.'

This seems to me unconvincing on two chief counts. First, Professor Fontenrose's demonstration of myth reads still more like a demonstration of wondertale and heroic legend. Second, the correspondences between the two stories are too general to be impressive. Nos. 2, 3, 4, 5, and 6 lack all urgency; nos. 8 and 12 would appear unavoidable in a story involving the deaths of two such protagonists; no. 7 I would relate to such heroic convention as we find in the *Battle of Maldon* rather than to folktale, much less myth; and no. 10 is a commonplace. This leaves no. 1, for which see the reference to the *Anglo-Saxon Chronicle* on p. 33 below; no. 9, whose second half is unremarkable; and no. 11, which requires special pleading.

Undoubtedly we need to widen our view of the structure of *Beowulf* if we accept that its two parts are variant expressions of the same myth. But I see no sign that such identification was ever in the poet's mind. For him Grendel and Grendel's Mother were one traditional set of supernatural adversaries, and the Dragon a different kettle of fish altogether.

Beowulf's best known foes. Bothvar Bjarki, declaredly a Bear's Son, fought with the living dead (maybe with one, the enigmatic Agnarr, certainly with an army of them at Lejre); with a winged monster at a foreign king's court (which he kills); and at a pinch he may be considered to have fought with a woman troll, Skuld, who at a further pinch may be considered to have killed *him*—matters dealt with in the third part of this book. Grettir, the hero of the fourteenth-century Icelandic *Grettis Saga Ásmundarsonar*, fought with *draugar* twice and with a trollwoman; he also went down into a cave under a waterfall and was betrayed by a helping companion whose task it was to safeguard the rope which should bring him back up again. The correspondences between those parts of *Beowulf* which tell of Beowulf's fight with Grendel and Grendel's Mother at Heorot in Denmark, and those parts of *Grettis Saga* which tell of Grettir's fight with Glam in Forsæludal and with the trollwife at Eyjardalsá in Bardardal in Iceland, are impressively close and universally acknowledged, and a further substantial body of analogues has been discovered in medieval saga and romance.[1] For example, *Bósa Saga ok Herrautðs, Hálfdans Saga Eysteinssonar, Harðar Saga ok Hólmverjar, Gullþóris Saga, Orms þáttr Stórólfssonar*, and *Samsons Saga Fagra* in the North, and the romance *Wigalois* farther south, all supply parallels sometimes close, sometimes not. Expectedly, when we are dealing with a widespread and enduring wondertale, partial reminiscence and residual detail will be found frequently and in many places.

But to stay with *Beowulf*: its author was seized of a body of wondertale (some of its features likewise observable in myth) whose shape and features and general development in a Germanic context we readily discern, and craftsman that he was he made good use of this to help produce the poem which is his masterpiece. That is, he committed himself to a hero who as a young man achieved two related monster-killings at the court of a foreign king, and as an old man achieved a monster-killing in his own and native land. This last achievement brought about his own death. His foe was a

---

[1] For translations see in particular G. N. Garmonsway and Jacqueline Simpson, *Beowulf and its Analogues*, 1968. See too G. V. Smithers, *The Making of Beowulf*, 1961, and Nora K. Chadwick, 'The Monsters and Beowulf', in *The Anglo-Saxons*, edited by Peter Clemoes, 1959, pp. 171–203.

dragon, and that this *draca* had physical affinities with *draugr* or *ketta* is not indicated.[1] Admittedly one would be troubled to draw the dragon in any detail,[2] but as much can be said of Grendel and Grendel's Mother. For a man who cannot have seen an original our poet does very well indeed. And the hero-monster confrontation is perfect. The dragon was in his right place, fulfilling his proper function (*Draca sceal on hlǽwe, frōd, frǽtum wlanc*: 'A dragon shall live in a mound, old and proud of his ornaments'). So too was Beowulf,

---

[1] G. V. Smithers in *The Making of Beowulf* argues strongly on different grounds from Professor Fontenrose that the dragon is a variant of the *draugr* or 'creature who haunts a grave-mound after death', and that in story-terms he is to be identified with the 'last survivor' who laid up in a mound the treasure he would henceforth watch over in the shape of a dragon. But the poem distinguishes between these two absolutely:

> So the sad-hearted man proclaimed his sorrows, lone survivor of them all, and wandered joyless day and night till death's tide touched at his heart. The old foe of the half-light found the joyous hoard standing open, he who seeks out barrows all afire, flies by night a naked nithdrake wrapped in flame—dwellers round about fear him greatly. He must seek a treasure in the earth where ancient in years he watches over the heathen gold—and is none the better off for it (2267–77).

Professor Smithers accepts that 'To the author of *Beowulf* it was no longer clear that the dragon was identical with the "last survivor" and therefore had been a human being.' Either the poet misunderstood this part of his story material or it was already blurred for him. I would put it more strongly: in *Beowulf* the last survivor is the last survivor, the dragon is a dragon, and the poet sees neither as anything else at any time. For him the dragon is not a *draugr*, and the second part of his poem is not a variant on Part One.

I offer two (I fear) unfairly brief comments on Professor Smithers' remarks on the unity of the poem (p. 12). That *Beowulf* is 'genetically' a unity follows, I think, from the circumstance that one and the same hero undertakes wonder-tale ridding-tasks against supernatural adversaries, whether we consider Grendel, Grendel's Mother, and the Dragon as *draugar* or not. The poem can be an 'aesthetic' unity only in so far as its unity is aesthetic, that is, apparent in terms of its own art form, and this, I suspect, cannot be demonstrated by finding a significance in the second part of the poem of which its poet was unaware.

[2] It is likely that the Germanic dragon owed something to the horse, and the representation of his head to a shrilling, grinning horsehead. His body seems to have been thought of as narrow and serpentlike. Our *Beowulf* dragon has been given one canine characteristic—the way in which from time to time he turns back into the barrow looking for his vanished treasure just as a dog turns back from time to time to where he knows he left his vanished bone (2293–300).

the people's guardian. That such dread veterans of the wars prove fatal to each other was a thing foredoomed, and the deaths of man and creature conclude a heroic story with heroic propriety.[1]

The fight and its preliminaries, as is usual with our poet, are formally deployed and heavily embellished. There is a deal of historical reference to hostilities between Geats and Swedes, Geats and Franks, whose significance is touched on below (see p. 33ff.); the deeply-troubled king discourses with an old man's wisdom of past events, present intentions, and future prospects; at a fitting time he delivers his *gilp*, his vaunting speech, as a hero should; we hear much of the dragon's treasure-hoard, its origins in sorrow and its enduring uselessness to men; and the Geat comitatus, that band of the king's chosen comrades who should rightly have died for him, is brought grievously to prominence by its cowardice and disloyalty. Conversely we watch a young hero, Beowulf's successor to the gift-stool of the Geats, bearing himself as a brave man should. The fight itself is soon over. With a huge iron shield made specially for the occasion the still mighty king, swelling with rage, shouts his challenge to the dragon inside his mound; the foe, three hundred years gold's guardian, quickly emerges, and the fight takes place in three desperate rounds. In the first Beowulf is forced to give ground; in the second he is so obviously getting the worse of it that his retainers flee to the shelter of a wood, and only Wiglaf hurries down to help his hard-pressed lord. In the third his sword snaps, the dragon bites him mortally in the neck, but Wiglaf pierces the dragon's unarmoured underbelly, and with the last of his strength the old man draws his sax and severs him at the middle. This is a handsome apportioning of glory for veteran and bachelor, nor is the firedrake without lurid splendour in life and a stricken majesty in death.

Beowulf's slayer lay there too, the dread earth-dragon, emptied of life and whelmed in ruin. No longer might the coiled serpent reign over his hoard of treasure, but the edges of swords, hard, battle-

[1] This is one of several contexts where the inquirer will be both wiser and better-informed if he re-reads J. R. R. Tolkien's 'Beowulf: The Monsters and the Critics' (Sir Israel Gollancz Memorial Lecture, British Academy, 1936).

notched, offspring of hammers, had demolished him, so that the far-flier sank to the ground near his treasure hall, stilled by his wounds. Not now did he wheel sporting in air at midnight, reveal his face exulting in riches, but he fell to earth through the might of the war-leader's hand (2824–35).

If we were now to summarize the story and substance of *Beowulf* along lines different from those of wondertale and Germanic heroic legend, and show that its bases and controls lay elsewhere, in myth (a task many times embarked on with results between the unlikely and the impossible),[1] or in northern history (a venture notoriously

---

[1] The most memorable lines of approach have been, I think, these:

(1) The Beow of the Anglo-Saxon genealogies, son of Scyld or Sceldwa and descendant of Sceaf (*bēow*, grain, barley: *scēaf*, sheaf), was apparently a god of agriculture and fertility. The first Beowulf of our poem (18–57 only), son of Scyld, a descendant of Scef, and father of Healfdene, may be identified with Beow. The stories of this Beow-Beowulf's struggles with monsters are the myths proper to a god of agriculture and fertility, and have in a manner unknown, a place unmarked, and a time unrecorded, been transferred to Beowulf son of Ecgtheow, who may therefore be seen as a divine person established in myth.

(2) The same Beow conducts as before to Beow-Beowulf, and so to the hero of our poem who is to be seen as a divine protector of mankind from the destructive forces of nature. Grendel is the spoiling sea, or more specifically the in-rushing spring-tides of the North Sea or, more recently, the Baltic; his Mother is the sea's hostile depth; the Dragon represents the onset of fierce weather towards winter, inimical and deathly. Or the nature-myths may be of marsh, swamp and fen, or the terror-haunted darkness of the northern night, tamed or defeated by sky-god, sun-god, weather-god, or such other god as Beowulf can be identified with.

(3) As vegetation-god and sun-god grow victims of our modern contagion of disbelief and fade from field and sky, the esoteric interpreters of *Beowulf* have taken fresh heart and new bearings, this time in the fields of pagan (Germanic) or Christian mythology. The reference points are Heorot-Asgard-Eden; Grendel's kin-the Jotuns-Moral Evil; Beowulf-Thor-Christ; Dragon-Midgarthsormr-Satan; with such additions as are yielded by Herebeald-Balder, Hama and the Brosinga mene, and the like. For a precise allegorical Christian interpretation see the footnote on p. 40 below, and for a comment p. xxiii above and pp. 48–9 below.

(4) There remains the detailed summary of *Beowulf* Part One, and the equation of *Beowulf* Part Two with *Beowulf* Part One (see pp. 16–17 n. above), made by Fontenrose, who sees Beowulf's fights with Grendel and Grendel's Mother, and thereafter his fight with the Dragon, as variants of a subtype of the combat myth which he traces through the ancient world in Europe and Asia from his starting-point in the Homeric Hymn to Apollo which records

self-defeating), we should at least answer the well-known stricture of some well-known critics that the *Beowulf* poet was so little the master of his material that he placed the irrelevancies (the monsters) at the poem's centre, and the serious things (the historical, pseudo-historical, and legendary elements) on its outer edges. The monsters are at the centre because the centre is their proper place. Granted that our author saw Beowulf as a king, and hero of a heroic poem, we cannot fail to see that behind this conventionally-accoutred figure falls the long shadow of the strong hero of folktale, wave-piercer, scourge of sea-beasts, cleanser of a house, grappler with a monstrous arm, finder of a wondrous sword, destroyer of giants and merewife, to say nothing of dragon-slayer later. It follows that we must accept *Beowulf* for what it is, and judge it by the canons of criticism appropriate to it. Had its author proposed to write an epic after the fashion of Homer, to withstand a summary after the fashion of Aristotle, he would have chosen a different hero, from a different milieu, and set him to different adventures. Had he proposed to re-count a myth of a divine being performing cosmic tasks he would not have made his god into a man achieving non-cosmic adventures. Had he proposed to write a historical poem, and we accept under that head historical tradition and legendary history, he would not have given his poem up to fabulous monsters and the achievement of non-historical tasks.

That said, we repeat that it was not our author's intention to repeat a folktale in folktale manner. Not only is our ignorance complete as to what version or versions of the monster stories counted most with him, but we cannot be sure to what extent he recognized the monster stories as different in kind from legendary and historical tradition. However, unless we are to assume without a shred of

---

that Apollo fought with a she-dragon, and in Simonides and the pseudo-Julian which record that Apollo killed a he-dragon named Python. We can be grateful to Professor Fontenrose for so eruditely displaying the Apollo-Python story as a possible area of reference for Germanic myth and wondertale; and once more we may agree that husks and sheddings of myth are discover-able in our poem; but his summary of *Beowulf* as myth seems to me on the whole to show that it is heroic legend and wondertale with remote and largely forgotten mythical antecedents for some of its features. Also there are numerous places where we do not read the poem in the same way.

3. DRAGONHEAD FROM A MIGRATION AGE SHIP
From the river Scheldt

evidence that some utterly vanished predecessor had already produced an utterly vanished version of the same story, and that our author merely retold it as he knew it—and a more arbitrary and unhelpful assumption could hardly be devised—unless we wander after will-o'-the wisps like this, it seems reasonable to conclude that he gratefully accepted the guiding lines of well-established folktales and the freedom to add non-folktale episodes and dissertations; established his story within the boundaries of a carefully portrayed heroic society, with the decisive changes of emphasis and tone sequent on such a transfer; for reasons we can guess at provided his hero with a geographical and historical setting; and gave story and hero a moral significance beyond the requirements or tolerance of folktale. So that if we at last proceed to summarize the poem as it presently exists we have the following:

I. Lines 1–2199. Young Beowulf in Denmark

The poem opens with the story of Scyld, the eponymous founder of the Danish Scylding dynasty, who came from over the sea a helpless child, and was returned to it after a glorious reign. His great-grandson king Hrothgar builds a mighty hall Heorot for magnificence and joy, but it is invaded by a monster in giant human form called Grendel, who kills no fewer than thirty men in each of his opening assaults, and by his continuing malignancy denies Hrothgar the use of his hall by night for twelve long years. Danish wisdom and valour alike avail nothing.

News of the king's affliction comes to the ears of Beowulf, the nephew of Hygelac, king of the Geats, and with the approval of his peers he makes a sea-journey to Heorot with fourteen chosen companions. Beowulf has, we are told, the strength of thirty men in his handgrip. In Denmark he declares his purpose, and is given an honourable welcome, except that during the feast that follows a Danish courtier named Unferth calls his skill and valour in question. By way of reply Beowulf tells how he outswam Breca in a seven-day swimming contest and slew nine monsters with his drawn sword. He vows that this time again he will conquer or die. And conquer by strength alone, without shield or sword.

As the shadows thicken the Danes retire from the hall, leaving

4. GILT-BRONZE DRAGON FROM THE SUTTON HOO SHIP BURIAL

its defence to Beowulf and his Geats. All save Beowulf fall asleep. He alone, when Grendel came stalking off the moors, sees him enter and devour a sleeping warrior.[1] He reaches for Beowulf, and they fight hand-to-hand until Beowulf tears the monster's arm off at the shoulder, and Grendel must flee, dying, to his fen-refuge. Men followed his tracks there the next morning, and as they returned the minstrel sang to them the contrasting tales of the hero Sigemund and his nephew Fitela and of the cruel and unhappy king Heremod. At Heorot all are joyful as they survey Beowulf's bloody trophy; there is oratory and feasting and a hero's reward for his deed. A minstrel tells the tragic tale of Finn. Queen Wealhtheow gives Beowulf precious gifts, including the torque which we are told king Hygelac the Geat would wear on his fatal expedition to Frisia. That evening the Danish chivalry re-occupies the hall.

Disastrously. This time Heorot is raided by Grendel's Mother, who in a night-scene of anguish and uproar carries off a Danish retainer and recovers her son's arm. Beowulf, who has been sleeping elsewhere, is summoned to the royal presence, heartens the Danes, and promises to track down the she-monster. He does so, accompanied by his Geats and a troop of Danes led by Hrothgar, and when they reach the blood-stained mere he plunges down alone to find her. He is attacked, but vainly, by sea-beasts as she grapples with him and drags him to her dwelling. The struggle in her underwater hall is hard and long; his sword, a choice weapon lent him by his earlier detractor Unferth, will not bite on her, and it is only when he has resort to a wondrous sword reposing in the lair itself that he prevails and kills her. He sees Grendel lying dead and cuts off his head. Meantime the discouraged Danes, seeing blood come up through the waters of the mere, take themselves off.[2] His own men stay on, sick at heart. He makes a safe return with Grendel's head

[1] That the companions shall fall sound asleep, and Beowulf make no move to prevent the devouring of his follower, are incidents inexplicable in the context of a heroic poem unless we recognize them for what they are: gaunt and unassimilable folktale motifs which the *Beowulf* poet found he could neither reject nor rationalize.

[2] Here, unlike the residual grotesqueries of the companions falling asleep at Heorot, and Beowulf watching Grendel devour his friend and retainer Hondscio, the poet has neatly rationalized, or used a rationalization of, the folktale motif of the deserting companions.

and the hilt of the wondrous sword, whose blade had melted away after contact with Grendel's venomous blood, and they make their way to Heorot with these spoils. Hrothgar makes a long descant on mutability and moderation, and the next morning Beowulf receives his promised reward and takes his leave.

Down at the shore the Geats load their ship with horses, weapons, and treasures, hoist sail, and proceed to their own country, their king Hygelac, and his queen Hygd. The poet discourses of Thryth (Modthrytho), who appears to have been a perilous maiden before marriage and a gracious queen thereafter. Beowulf tells Hygelac about his adventures, and is led to speculate on what must be the ill consequences of a proposed dynastic marriage between Hrothgar's daughter Freawaru and Froda's son, the Heathobeard prince Ingeld. He then bestows on Hygelac and Hygd the gifts he had received from king Hrothgar and queen Wealhtheow. Despite the doubts suggested by his unprofitable youth (which we now hear mentioned for the first time) he has shown himself glorious, and Hygelac rewards him with his own father's sword, a vast estate, a hall, and a princely throne.

II. Lines 2200–3182. *Beowulf's Fight with the Dragon*

After the death in battle of Hygelac and his son Heardred, Beowulf became king over the Geats and ruled them well for fifty years, till one of his subjects stole a precious cup from a dragon's treasure-hoard and the dragon visited his vengeance upon the country-side.

Old now, troubled in mind, yet valiant as ever, Beowulf determines to protect his people and meet the dragon in single combat. He has a shield of iron (it would require the strength of thirty men to manage it) made to this end, and while he awaits battle reviews past history: the slaughter of Hygelac and his Geats on a raid into Frisia, from which Beowulf alone escaped by a stupendous feat of swimming; the death of Heardred at the hands of the Swedes, and of king Haethcyn before him; the cruel mishaps which had brought Hygelac to the throne in the first place; Beowulf's role as Hygelac's champion; his clash with Grendel. He tells his eleven companions that this time too he will win fame or death.

He now challenges the dragon to come out and fight. It is a sore encounter. One only of his companions comes to his aid, young Wiglaf; despite his reminding them of the obligations owed to loyalty, gratitude, reputation, and love, the other ten flee into the forest. Beowulf and Wiglaf kill the dragon when he makes his third onset, but Beowulf is hurt to death. He has just time to see the dragon's treasure before he dies.

Wiglaf announces his death to the cowards and bitterly reproves them a second time. A messenger reminds the main body of the Geats of the ill-will existing between them and the Franks since Hygelac's time, and surveys the long history of the Geat-Swedish wars. Nothing but disaster lies ahead for the Geat people. At Wiglaf's command they prepare Beowulf's funeral pyre, celebrate his obsequies, and erect a mighty barrow over their well-loved king.

2. Heroic Legend and Legendary History

CLEARLY *BEOWULF* IS A COMPLEX POEM, AND SUCH BY intention. The contests with Grendel and Grendel's Mother in Part One, and that with the Dragon in Part Two, dictate its shape and control its progression, but in both the literal and metaphorical sense they are by no means the whole of the story. The so-called 'digressions and episodes' take up almost a quarter of the poem's length, affect its tone and substance, and powerfully enhance its heroic and elegiac quality. They are of several kinds, and some of them, to a modern eye, hang loosely on their hinges. It would be arrogant not to allow that the modern eye may be bright with modern error. For all we know it was the eighth-century audience's expectation that it would be treated to these interruptions, digressions, amplifications; and would listen to them with the gratification due to an effect of art foreseen. 'Listened' is the key word, for reading was a rare and arcane practice when *Beowulf* was composed and for a long while thereafter. For the majority the poem was read, recited, or intoned aloud, and we assume that the voice and art of its deliverer would receive a measure of support from lyre or harp. A sudden transition is one thing on the printed page and quite another at a live performance where voice, harp, presence, mien, and the controlling authority of an artist can (and in our common experience do) so impose themselves upon us, so command our eye and ear, that cloister-problems are not seen, and closet-doubts not heard. The poem's exclamatory opening, the transition from praise of Sigemund to regret after Heremod (pp. 31–2), our induction into the tale of Finn (1063 ff), the abrupt switch from the wise and gentle Hygd, bride of Hygelac and queen of the Geats, to the cruel-

hearted Thryth, bride of Offa and queen of the Angles, the pre-
emptive shift from Part One to Part Two and the introduction of
the Dragon, are challenges inviting solutions by a resourceful
trained performer. And not only solutions—enhancements. The
poem supplies its own example of such exultant virtuosity, when
Beowulf recounts in Hygelac's court how Hrothgar, old, brave, and
wise, touched the harp in joy and sorrow, and chanted for his guests'
entertainment something of mirth, something of grief, now a lay
both bitter and true, now a tale of wonders, now a descant on his
vanished youth and one-time strength in battle (2105–14). Exhortation, transition, fresh arrivals and new departures, changes of mood
and extensions of reference, played as essential a part in a performance of *Beowulf* as aria and recitative, solos and choruses, and changes
of costume and scenery in a nineteenth-century opera. With the
addendum that a poem of over 3000 lines, composed that it might
be heard, required breaks in structure and acceptable rest-points. We
should not be afraid to conclude that our author knew better than
we what he was doing.

    And yet for today's reader a problem remains, and by readers
insulated from oratory and oral entertainment is felt to be acute.
They are pleased to read news of the newsworthy Thryth, but
would be still more pleased to read it in some poetic fragment
devoted to her particular story rather than in *Beowulf*, where even
if they can be intellectually convinced of the propriety of her appear-
ing at all, her entry appears so sudden, clumsy, and violent that
despairing scholars have been reduced to postulating a hiatus in the
text and denying a much-maligned lady the spelled-out letters of
her name. We can all agree that this is the author's most flagrant
example of 'dragging in the Romans', but the varying significance
found by different readers in the passages about Sigemund,
Heremod, and the trouble at Finnesburg, does not encourage a
belief that they, and they alone, are necessary to the poem and
fully integrated with it. Another hero, another villain, a different
tale of irreconcilable loyalties—Ragnarr who killed a dragon,
Eormenric who had a wolfish mind, Theodoric who held the
Mærings' stronghold—would these not do as well? And Waldhere
and his Hildigund, Maethhild and her love-devoured Geat, the

holocausts at Bravellir and Lejre, or the wars of the Huns and Goths, would these have been worse, though probably no better? The questions are rhetorical and require no answer. We must trust our poet and declare our willingness to keep with him. The blame is on time and lapsed memory if in places we read *Beowulf* more aware of its matter than its structural art, and even then must sometimes wonder what we are reading, and why.

As to why, there must be an answer. The legendary and historical sections are there for a purpose, sometimes precise and apposite, sometimes to be guessed at. We believe that the poem was a consciously literary work addressed to a well-informed audience with known expectations. Between them the literary ambitions of the author and the aural expectations of his audience ensured that *Beowulf* would be both more than and different from the 'wild folk-tale' which a less sophisticated collaboration might have produced. Poet and audience were familiar with the heroic traditions of their race: traditions which had attached themselves to many famous men, a few famous women, and were sometimes still in process of being attached to names which might in time become famous. No small proportion of this heroic tradition was itself emergent from wondertale (for example, the mysterious coming and no less mysterious departure of Scyld, the gabbing between Beowulf and Unferth over the swimming-contest with Breca, Thryth as perilous maiden, and much of what we hear about the Dragon, his riches, and his slaying), and in the technical sense had risen to a heroic level of story in that it had become attached to a named hero. That a poet with entertainment and instruction in mind should amplify his main theme by recourse to these traditions would appear, in the absence of conclusive evidence to the contrary, the most natural thing in the world. To our present (and one imagines unaugmentable) knowledge there was no heroic legend associated with Beowulf of the Geats.[1] The aura of epic must come from elsewhere. Beowulf

[1] It has been many times remarked that the characters, events, and setting of this very English poem are not English. There is nothing surprising about this. The chief repositories of common Germanic tradition were continental not insular; the great majority of named heroes belonged there. If we are to judge by the rest of Old English heroic or elegiac verse we might guess that had more Old English 'epic' compositions been preserved they would be

must be shown to be of the calibre of the Waelsing-Volsung champions Sigemund and Fitela (Sigmund and Sinfjotli), of Finn who ruled the Frisians and Hnaef and Hengest who captained the Half-Danes. Offa and Ingeld, the one a hero-king, 'best of all mankind between the seas', the other a hero-prince of the Heathobards and Froda's gracious son, are introduced into the poem as his peers. All such, whatever else they are, are proof of his stature and avouchment of his worth. They make him more than the third prince or youngest son of folktale; they are his contemporary letters of credit; they guarantee his place. The tale of Ingeld establishes his political sagacity, his reading of men and affairs, his fitness to rule; the story of Sigemund who killed a dragon and rescued a treasure, and, though our poem does not say so, died fighting against impossible odds, and not without thought for the future of the Volsungs, has by many scholars been held prophetic for Beowulf who will also kill a dragon and rescue a treasure, and die fighting against impossible odds with his last thoughts on his people and successor. One would like to agree, but the passage is equally entertaining if considered part of the minstrel's repertoire, a tale brought naturally to mind by Beowulf's destruction of Grendel, a capping anecdote and enhancing recall, rather than a portent or deliberate parallel. It is introduced naturally enough. The king's thanes who have followed Grendel's tracks to the mere, and discovered in its bloody waters proof of his death, return home rejoicing. As they ride along they are full of Beowulf's praises, nor did they speak anything but good of their own king Hrothgar.

Sometimes the famed warriors let their bay steeds gallop, go racing where the track looked good to them and was known for its excellence.

---

found to concern themselves with other continental heroes such as Waldhere, Theodoric, Sigmund, Starkad, and their like. Alcuin might ask what Ingeld had to do with Christ; but an Old English court audience would not ask what he had to do with them. They were as clear on this score as English, Norman, French, German story-tellers and audiences would later be about what the British Arthur and his Celtic ménage had to do with *them*. Similarly the heroes of the Icelandic *Fornaldar Sögur* were not Icelanders, nor necessarily even Scandinavians: they could belong with Rhine and Danube, Burgundian realm or country of the Goths.

Sometimes a king's thane, a man laden with eloquence, his mind
charged with story, who remembered so many things of old, devised
new matter, bound truly in verse—began to set forth Beowulf's
exploit with skill, successfully to tell a fitting tale, ring changes on
words. He related well-nigh everything that he had heard tell of
Sigemund's mighty deeds, the Waelsing's struggle, his journeyings
far and wide, and many a thing unknown, feuds and deeds of violence
which the children of men would have no knowledge of had not Fitela
been with him when he wished to tell of such, the uncle to his
nephew, for they had always been comrades at need in every trial,
and put many of the monster race to the sword.

No little glory arose for Sigemund after his deathday, since the
brave warrior had killed the dragon, the treasure's guardian. The
prince's son ventured on the perilous deed alone, in under the grey
rock—Fitela was not with him. Even so it was granted that the lordly
iron, his sword, pierced the wondrous serpent, stuck fast in the rock.
The dragon's death was violent. The champion had ensured by his
prowess that he might dispose of the ring-hoard even as he wished.
Waels's son loaded his sea-boat, bore the bright ornaments into the
bosom of the ship: the dragon melted in its own heat. Because of his
brave deeds the safeguard of warriors was the most widely renowned
of adventurers throughout the nations of men—in days of old he
throve by virtue of that—once Heremod's warring slackened, his
strength and valour (864–902).

There is no questioning the interest of this, with its reminder
that in English tradition it was Sigemund and not his son Sigurd
who was famous as a dragon-killer; and there is no questioning its
aptness in the mouth of the scop as Danes and Geats ride home to
Heorot. What can be questioned, in a properly dispassionate way,
is whether we should seek a more loaded reference and deeper
structural significance. Since we know that our poet does look
forward at times, both by hint, as in his reference to the eventual
destruction of Heorot by fire (81–5 and 778–82), and by direct
statement, as in his first striking reference to the death in Frisia of
the torque-adorned Hygelac (1202–14, see p. 58), we should not be
over-hasty in denying a planned relevance here too. This leaves us,
even so, a long way short of postulating a theory of Old English
poetical composition analogous with the interlace designs common

in Anglo-Saxon visual art. In the passage just quoted, for example, we move from Sigemund to Heremod for entirely practical reasons. Our poet is not a beginner. He had his professional repertoire of reference and device, including all such poetic counters as might forward a theme of valour, pride, tyranny, monster-ridding, perilous maidenhood, faithlessness or the repayment of mead, and deployed it professionally. Heremod was an exemplar much to his purpose (he would use him a second time to give point to Hrothgar's discourse to Beowulf on manly virtue (1709–24)), and after the deceptively casual reference to him that closes the eulogy of Sigemund he goes on to speak of him in a professional's conventional and telling way—still through the mouth of the minstrel. Such things were part of his training, his factual equipment, and his poetic technique: he needed a gloomy tyrant, and Heremod supplied the need.

He [Heremod] was betrayed forth among the Eotenas, into the power of his foes, speedily dispatched to his death. Rising sorrows oppressed him too long; he became a lifelong anxiety to his people, to all the athelings. Moreover in days gone by many a wise man who had looked to him for comfort in trouble—that the king's son should prosper, succeed to his father's rank and virtue, protect the people, the treasure and the stronghold, that kingdom of heroes, the Scyldings' homeland—many such mourned the brave-hearted man's departure. Hygelac's kinsman brought more happiness to his friends, to all mankind; but violence entered [Heremod's] heart (902–15).

If there is more than a generalized comparison of Beowulf and Sigemund in the first part of the minstrel's lay, might we not expect to find a more than generalized contrast between Beowulf and Heremod in the second? The question is one to which we are unlikely to find more than a generalized answer. The poet's use of a story rooted in wondertale, and therefore of a hero who in discharging wondertale tasks must necessarily have a wondertale aura, together with his achievement in maintaining both tale and hero at Germanic epic level by his use of heroic legend, history, historical tradition, and didactic material, is explanation enough of the episodes and digressions, whose content and placing sometimes appear open to variation, or even to improvement—though in respect of these last we may recognize that we are in a poor position to judge, and a worse to pass harsh sentence.

In respect of his more 'historical' material—that is, when he recounts the historical traditions of the Danes, Geats, and Swedes, whether they are true history or not—our author's purpose appears clear and well-founded. Still, three caveats must be entered straightaway. There is not a shred of evidence for a historical Beowulf; most of what we are told about the Geat-Swedish wars has been and remains the subject of sharp dispute and rival interpretation; and we are not sure how far, if at all, the poet distinguished between legendary and historical references. Was Scyld, for instance, less real to him than Hrothgar, Ingeld than Hygelac? We shall never know. Just as we shall never know whether Grendel was less real to him (factually, not imaginatively) than Hrothulf, who as Hrolf Kraki is decidedly unreal to us today; or Grendel's perilous mother than Offa's perilous maiden. One suspects he had an order of belief, but one less inhibited than ours. He had scriptural authority for the existence of evil spirits, giants, and monsters, all such as were of Cain's seed. If fiery dragons could intrude into the *Anglo-Saxon Chronicle* for the year 793,[1] why should they not be accommodated in an Anglo-Saxon poem of comparable age and dignity? Even today, with scepticism at its height, the one thing harder to prove than the existence of Hrolf-Hrothulf in early sixth-century Denmark and Finn in mid-fifth-century Frisia is their non-existence; and in eighth-century England or thereabouts it would not have occurred to poets, minstrels, genealogists, antiquaries, and other such purveyors of tradition, to seek to prove either. They and their fabled like belonged to the corpus of knowledge, were accepted and fully believed in.

Yet the two areas of historical material to which the *Beowulf* poet refers most frequently, Hygelac's expedition to Frisia (five times)

[1] 'In this year terrible portents appeared over Northumbria and sadly affrighted the inhabitants: these were exceptional flashes of lightning, and fiery dragons were seen flying in the air. A great famine followed soon upon these signs, and a little after that in the same year on the ides of January [*read* June] the harrying of the heathen miserably destroyed God's church in Lindisfarne by rapine and slaughter.'

and the Geat-Swedish wars (six times), are significantly different from all the other episodes in that Beowulf is held to have played a part in them. It is true that he says he had met Freawaru, the bride of Ingeld, in her father's hall, Heorot, but this is merely the cue for his thoughtful presumption of one more Danish-Heathobeard disaster. But he accompanied Hygelac on his death-raid into Frisia, fought alongside him against the Franks, and alone of Geats came safely off the field. The raid and Hygelac's death c. 521 are helpfully attested in sources that know nothing of Beowulf, the *Historia Francorum* of Bishop Gregory of Tours (d. 594), the anonymous eighth-century *Liber Historiae Francorum*, and a curious English book of the eighth century whose subject is monsters and strange beasts, *Liber Monstrorum* or *De Monstris et de Belluis*. Between them these inform us how a king named Ch(l)ochilaicus-Huiglaucus-Hyglac(us) made a piratical raid on the lands of the Attuarii (the *Hetware* of *Beowulf* 2363, 2916), a Frankish people living under the protection of the Merovingian king between the lower Rhine and the Zuyder Zee. Here he plundered a village and carried the booty out to his ships. Hygelac himself remained on shore, where he was trapped and killed by an army led by Theudobert, son of the Frankish king Theudoric. Thereafter his fleet was routed and his booty restored to its owners. The skeleton (*ossa*) of king Huiglaucus, who ruled the Geats (? *qui imperavit Getis*), a man so huge that from the age of twelve no horse could carry him (a comparable vastness would later be attributed to Göngu-Hrólfr, Hrolf the Walker, Rollo the founder of the dukedom of Normandy), was preserved on an island at the mouth of the Rhine, and long displayed as a marvel of the human creation. The two Frankish chroniclers refer to Ch(l)ochilaicus as king of the Danes, which need not surprise us, and to Beowulf they refer not at all, which should surprise us still less. For down in Frisia he looks very much the folktale hero, the Bear's Son, who hugs his chief adversary to death, then plunges into the sea and swims the long way home, with thirty suits of armour hung about him. 'It was not the sword that slew him,' says the poem, 'but my warlike grasp crushed his body, the beatings of his heart.' And again: 'Beowulf escaped there through his own strength, used his power of swimming, had all alone thirty suits of armour on his arm when he plunged into the sea. . . . The son of Ecgtheow swam back to his people across the sea's expanse, grief-stricken and solitary' (2359–68).

Nor is he mentioned in any outside record of the Geat-Swedish wars. The military and dynastic details, as these are recounted in northern prose and poetry, are striking in themselves but not arguable in our present context; the accuracy of the details need not now concern us, nor the major uncertainties of who is who and what is what. Whether we regard the Geats as the Jutes, which is possible, or the Gautar resident in Sweden below the great lakes, which is probable; or accept the dismissive theory that they are a fictional product of legendary history and mythological geography; whether we go along with *Ynglinga Saga*, *Skjöldunga Saga*, or the *Historia Norwegiae*; whatever significance we attach to the Swedish parallels to Sutton Hoo and their relevance for *Beowulf*; and into whichever century we fit the subjection of the Gautar by the Swedes, re-membering that good cases have been argued for the sixth, ninth, and even the tenth; make what we will of all this, we are still left without a straw's weight of evidence for Beowulf the man.[1] Beowulf the king stands in even worse case. He suffers from a double dis-ability. There is no corroborative evidence that he existed, and as though this is not enough, he could not be fitted into northern history if he did. His fifty year reign conforms to a story-teller's need, and is not to be believed in.

Yet, while these hard sentences about the non-historicity of the man Beowulf needed saying, they do nothing to shake our earlier statement (on p. 33 above) about the propriety of the *Beowulf* poet's frequent and sustained use of the legendary history and historical tradition of the Danes, Geats, and Swedes. This was legitimate, purposeful, and advantageous to his poem and hero alike.

First we might postulate that our poet portrayed Beowulf as a member of the Geat ruling house because he knew no better, and that for him there was a northern hero of that name. That he fought

---

[1] These matters have been exhaustively but still not conclusively argued by many scholars in many languages, of whom R. W. Chambers in English and the Weibulls in Swedish appear to me the most important. I have attempted a brief conspectus in my *History of the Vikings*, pp. 34–44.

against the Franks and Frisians, and eventually against the Swedes, and that 'when Hygelac fell, and war-swords brought death to Heardred under his protecting shield, when the War-Scylfings, harsh war-wolves, attacked him among his victorious people, brought low in battle the nephew of Hereric—after all this the broad kingdom came into the hands of Beowulf' (2201–8)—these were the facts as he knew them. Second, we might assume, altogether less convincingly, that our poet had sufficient knowledge of these far-off things and battles long ago to realize that their known outlines, suspected lacunae, and imprecision in matters of detail made them the ideal setting for an interpolated hero. For who should say these things were not so? Either way he lodged his hero more securely in his audience's mind by making him a man of their own kind, not only a killer of monsters and attracter of heroic reference, but one who had sat in hall, heard minstrels, taken gifts at a lord's hand, and when the mead must be paid for did battle for king and people, glory and riches, against such realizable adversaries as Franks and Frisians and the martial Swedes. These were things that brought him home to men's bosoms, for these were the things they had done or were prepared to do themselves. He was now more than a wheel of story, and appears the highborn, socially secure hero of an aristocratic poem composed for an hierarchical audience, for whom he provided not merely entertainment, but assurance, self-aware-ness, identification, and instruction. For example, immediately after the lines which tell us how Beowulf swam north from the mouths of the Rhine, then along the West Jutland coast to Skagen and so to Geatland, with thirty suits of armour on his arm, thus rounding off one of his most bearlike exploits, the poem moves into what is at once a sober and factual resumé of traditional historical events and an object lesson in the duties and obligations of even the greatest retainer.

The son of Ecgtheow swam back to his people across the sea's expanse, grief-stricken and solitary. There Hygd [Hygelac's young widow] offered him the treasure and the kingdom, riches and a throne. She did not trust to her son that he would know how to defend the royal seats against armies from outside, now that Hygelac was dead. But none the more for that could the bereaved people find it anywhere in the atheling's heart that he should become Heardred's overlord, or consent to take up royal power. Rather he upheld him among his people with friendly counsel, kindly and honourably, until he grew up and ruled the Geats.

Kinsmen in exile, the sons of Ohthere, came seeking his aid across the water. They had rebelled against the helm of the Scylfings [king Onela], the best of those sea-kings who broke out treasure in Sweden, a glorious prince.[1] This led to Heardred's death. In return for his hospitality Hygelac's son received as his lot a mortal wound from the swing of a sword. When Heardred had fallen, Ongentheow's son [Onela] set off back to regain his own home, and let Beowulf keep the throne and rule the Geats. He was a good king.

In later years he planned requital for the people's loss, befriended the hapless Eadgils, supported Ohthere's son across the wide water with an army, warriors and weapons. He took vengeance thereafter in cold, bitter campaigns, deprived Onela of life (2367–96).

One sentence later we are with the dragon. But though we, learned in our day and generation, may feel that the poet's craftmanship was not always equal to the task of dovetailing history and tradition into a wondertale and hero-tale design, he and his audience would have no such reservations, and, to leave theory for practice, and what might have been for what is, his engrossment with legend and history raises his poem to levels of dignity and significance it would otherwise hardly have attained.

And that in two ways. First, the historical reference is much richer in Part Two of the poem, and we ask ourselves why. A number of scholars whom we know to be mild, humane men, the very stuff one would think of which dragon-lovers are made, express themselves coldly, not to say straitly, on the hot and twisted firedrake destroyed at such cost by Beowulf and Wiglaf. The creature is commonplace, they inform us, the fight tedious— the writer, or even the reader, could do better himself, as wordsmith or fire-fighter. A cynic might wonder whether the poet took an equally poor view of dragon-fights, and buttressed what would otherwise be Beowulf's sagging dignity with his reminders of

[1] These events and personalities are touched on again in our Part Three, 'King Hrolf's Saga', p. 130 below.

Hygelac (and Beowulf) in Frisia (four of the five references in Part Two) and of the Swedish wars (all six in Part Two). In fact one is sure this was not so. One suspects it is likelier that our poet, knowing his business pretty well, kept these historical passages for their proper place, where they account for Beowulf's succession to the gift-stool of the Geats, partly fill in the otherwise yawning gap of his life between his monster-killings in Denmark and his dragon-fight at home, improve the poem's claim to epic status, and help ensure its magnificent close. In Part Two the Geats are a beleaguered people, with only Beowulf's right arm between them and disaster. They have the ill-will of the Franks, the hostility of the Swedes. Temporarily, but decisively, they have the conflagratory out-breathings of the dragon. Beowulf rids them of this last threat at the cost of his own life, and the Geats never doubt what is fated to follow. The glory of the Storm-lovers is over. They will now fall prey to their enemies the Swedes, as history, for all its chronological uncertainties, confirms that they did. The Geats were defeated, oppressed, uprooted, and absorbed. This is the poem's prognostication of the people's woe:

No warrior shall flaunt treasure in his memory, no lovely girl wear torque round her throat, but heavy-hearted and stripped of her gold shall tread not once but many a time the paths of exile, now that our army-leader has laid aside laughter, merriment and mirth. Because of this many a spear, cold at morning, shall be caught up and hefted in hand. No sweet song of the harp shall bid the warrior awake, but the dark raven, eager for doomed men, will discourse at large, tell the eagle how he fared at the banquet when along with the wolf he stripped the bodies of the slain (3015–27).

These are terms of foreboding that outreach the consequences of a dragon-fight. They add their own gloomy majesty to the poem's close, where a hero, king, dynasty, people, are seen sinking in ruin together.

Second, the acceptance of Beowulf by poet and audience as a historical person was a powerful reinforcement of the poem's morality. Without severing him from the world of wondertale entertainment, it set him alongside them in the world they knew,

5. SPLENDOUR OF GOLD, I. *Above* THE ÅLLEBERGNECK-RING; *below*: THE SUTTON HOO PURSE-LID.

with its fighting-men, thanes, counsellors in hall and owners of estates, with their dues and obligations, sanctions and rights. One should never seek to be exclusionist about a poet's aims, but the *Beowulf* poet was pursuing two main objectives: to entertain and instruct. He had few problems with the first: in the hands of a good story-teller Beowulf's exploits in Denmark, his warlike deeds thereafter, and his fight with the Dragon could hardly fail to interest—as interest they do to this day. His ideas of construction seem not to be those of his critics, more particularly the uncompromising way he brings in supporting material from heroic legend, his proneness to repetition (the Hygelac material, for example), his piecemeal deployment of the Swedish wars, and the either superbly self-possessed or naïvely primitive transition from Part One to Part Two; or in a different kind, his vagueness as to Grendel's physical dimensions, and such self-contradictions as affect our notion of Beowulf's active or sluggish youth and the nature and fate of the dragon's treasure. Yet with it all he holds the modern reader's attention no less commandingly than we believe he held his listener's in the days gone by. Thus the harkings-back to Hygelac's death in Frisia, as we have just said, are factually and emotionally cumulative in respect of Beowulf's wondertale characteristics and heroic exploits, emphasize his loyalty and judgement, explain his retributive intervention in the Swedish wars, and the harsh significance of an enduring Frankish ill-will. The refusal to define the size and aspect of Grendel, so that like his Mother (and like Ysbaddaden Penkawr in *Culhwch and Olwen*) he is what the story requires him to be at each particular moment, if logistically wrong is poetically right. That the valour and keenness of young Beowulf are stressed when we look for an appointed hero, and the youthful sloth and awkwardness characteristic of *kolbítr* and Bear's Son mentioned only when he has given proof of himself, whether by accident or design operates most happily for hero and reader. We learn that the dragon's treasure is girt about with spells, fatal and accurst, only after its acquiring has led to Beowulf's death, and may legitimately consider that we should have been informed of this before; but the poet, one suspects, would be unrepentant. With every allowance made for his narrative conventions, he will be found a good deal less than perfect, but

6. DRAGONFIGHT: SIGURD KILLS FAFNIR
From Hyllestad

once we are content to move with him on his own terms we find
that many so-called faults were in fact enhancements for his knowledgeable eighth-century audience, and no disadvantage to his
informed audience today.

And he was more than a well-trained teller of tales in well-
turned verse. Indeed there is so much moral teaching in the poem,
so pervasive a didactic purpose, that there has been speculation
whether it was written as a mirror for kings, *ad usum delphini*, a
slanted commentary on human weal and woe for a self-congratula-
tory band of escapist Christian brothers in a monastery, or a sermon
on the imperfections of the Germanic pagan heroic ideal directed at
would-be heroes in a royal hall. As to the first and second of these,
in that their intention is laudatory, one might agree that any eighth-
century king, uncorrupted by modesty and theology, would be
pleased to look into *Beowulf* and see his own face there; but as to the
third and fourth, with their assumption that the poet is critical of
his hero, surely the rockbottom, the *meregrund*, of Beowulfian
interpretation has been reached by those over-earnest explorers who
see in this noble and beneficent helm of the helpless the eighth
century's own particular anti-hero, and read the noble and dignified
and majestically explicit poem of action, elegy, and practical ideal-
ism which tells his story as a cunningly savoured cautionary tale
with an adder's sting in its last line.[1]

And there is a third, compelling reason why our poet presents us

---

[1] Because it is a work of art *Beowulf* not only challenges us to understand but
compels us to feel. It follows that however learned we become, however
fortified with our private editorial apparatus, we shall not attain, nor should
we seek to attain, a sterile objectivity of approach. We *must* react to it in our
own way; and if any reader feels that the *Beowulf* poet is critical of his hero,
and in the end sees his death as well-deserved because he has grown arrogant,
in love with worldly fame, is too much and too consciously the army-leader,
gold-giver, and shepherd of his people, is in short a 'deluded old man',
whether from good motives or bad, proud, greedy, scornful of God's help and
the support of his retainers, the blundering wrecker of his country's hopes—
he has been seen of late as all these things, as well as, at the opposite extreme,
an allegory of the Saviour whose three folktale adventures represent the
salvation of man, Christ's resurrection and the harrowing of hell, and Christ's
death—all one can do is notice the violent contradictions of these theories,
and express surprise that a poet who impresses us as level-headed and resourceful so signally failed to make his purpose clear.

with historical material. Germanic heroic poetry customarily derives from or is associated with an historical event or personage, from Hildebrand and the battle of the Goths and the Huns, by way of Sigurd-Siegfried, Theodoric and Ermanaric, to Byrhtnoth and his fyrd at Maldon; and the *Beowulf* poet could not be expected to evade this obligation of his art.

3. Heroic Virtue

ADMIRERS OF *BEOWULF* AND DR JOHNSON TOO MUST GIVE thanks that the Lives of the Poets started with Cowley. And yet one of that unflinching moralist's most emphatic pronouncements applies very well to this ancient and earnest poem. 'The end of writing is to instruct: the end of poetry is to instruct by pleasing.' The *Beowulf* poet wished to do both these things. As to instruction, there is the nature of his hero, and the nature of the supporting cast; there is the code of conduct extolled at all stages of the action; there are the overt dissertations on virtuous behaviour; and the poet's numerous comments on men and events. Hrothgar preaches against arrogance and heedlessness; Beowulf takes comfort that he is no oath-breaker, has never injured his kin, has pursued his country's well-being and defended it from oppression. Wiglaf is eloquent on the duties of the comitatus; and the poet is ever ready with commendations of his models: 'That was a good king'; 'He was a fine man'; 'Such shall a thane be'; 'They were a worthy people'. Or conversely: 'He was a heavy burden to his people' (of Heremod); 'Such is not a queenly (*or* womanly) custom for a lady to practise' (of Thryth). As we noted earlier (p. 4), we are plainly bidden to know what manly virtue is. The great questions are indirectly propounded and directly answered. 'What makes a man good?' 'What should we seek to be?' Because these are questions which every worthwhile human being has asked himself since the world began, and will continue to ask until the world ends, it follows that the poem's answers are relevant to worthwhile men today.

Yet every age, except for its recessions into self-indulgence, self-abasement, or self-pity, judges itself superior to its predecessors;

and in our modern sophistication we may be tempted to regard the code of conduct advanced by the *Beowulf* poet as over-simplified or rudimentary. It rests on the following values: bravery both physical and of the spirit (perhaps we should say valour, fortitude, and endurance); loyalty and service; generosity and reward; love of good fame; wisdom in the affairs of private and corporate life; and piety towards a god. These may be set out in any order and are capable of sub-division. We could go on to open a second list: etiquette and decorum; courtesy towards women; a regard for the physically beautiful; a love of splendour as this is revealed in the appurtenances of a lordly life: fine swords and brooches, fine horses, fine cups to drink from and fine halls to drink in, the intricate craft of a minstrel and the orator's breast-searching art. But the first list, valour, loyalty, fortitude, generosity, wisdom, and piety, is the more distinctive.

Beowulf is the fully valorous man. He is brave physically, just as fearless in combat when arrows shock over the shieldwall and the foot-fighters clash as when Grendel's steel-tipped claw thrusts at the halldoor or the twisted firedrake comes on a third time carrying blast and venom in his jaws. In all his life he has never drawn back for threat or peril. 'Wyrd (Fate) often spares an undoomed man when his courage holds good.' It is a hero's duty to preserve his life by valour; and valour, Beowulf tells us, has brought him safe through many perils, times of war. He is brave in another way. In his role of hero he is schooled to accept his destiny, whatever this may be. Fate, say the pagan poets, is immeasurably strong, all-powerful, and implacable. Man is at its mercy. 'Wyrd goes ever as it must.' Yet this in no way makes him weak and small. For if he accepts what is destined, without bowing to it, he triumphs over it. An unbreakable will makes him the equal of all-powerful Fate, and though Fate can destroy him, it can neither conquer nor humiliate him. If there are monsters to fight, fight them. If there is hardship to bear, bear it. If grief, endure. Evade nothing; complain of nothing. In all circumstances, at all times, a man must give of his best.

Without loyalty the social structure cannot hold. A leader owed it to his men, retainers owed it to their lord. Beowulf is a shining exemplar at either level. During Hygelac's lifetime he was his staunchest support. It was as Hygelac's man that he fought against Grendel in Denmark. It was by Hygelac's life that Hrothgar conjured him to fight with Grendel's Mother. It was of his followers and his lord that he spoke to 'the famous son of Healfdene' before setting off for the mere. 'If battle carries me off, be a protector to my young retainers, my close comrades. Likewise, beloved Hrothgar, send those treasures you have given me to Hygelac. Hrethel's son, the Geats' lord, may see then by that gold, as he gazes on the treasure, that I found a good and noble ring-giver, enjoyed his bounty while I might' (1480–86). In the event he conveys them to Hygelac himself, renders them up in love and duty, and in return is given the gold-decked sword of Hygelac's dead father, seven thousand in land, a hall and princely throne. Wherefore, 'There was no need for him to seek among the Gifthas or the Spear-Danes or the people of the Swedes for a champion less good than I, buy him for money. At all times I would be before him in the host, alone in the forefront, and ever will wage battle so, so long as this sword shall last, which early and late so oft has done me service, since I killed Daeghrefn champion of the Franks with my own hands in the presence of the army' (2494–502). As with Hygelac, so with Hygelac's young son. While he lived Beowulf upheld him among his people, would not take the proffered throne himself, and when he was killed took vengeance for him (see p. 37 above). The gloomy tyrant and faithless retainer, these are the rogues and deviants on whom the poet's judgement falls, in sorrow as in anger. Better die, perish in the dragon's fire, says Wiglaf, than bear shield back home in shame when one's dear lord has suffered and sunk in the fray. 'Death is better for any man than a life of reproach.'

This is part of the exhortation the young hero addresses to his craven comrades:

I remember that time we took mead, when we promised our lord in the beer-hall, him who gave us these treasures, that we would repay him this war-gear, these helms and hard swords, if need such as this befell him . . . Now the day has arrived when our lord has need of the strength of good fighting-men . . . For my part, God knows, I had much rather that the fire should swallow up my body along with my gold-giver. It does not seem right to me that we carry our

shields back home again, unless we can first fell the foe, protect the
life of the lord of the Weders (2633–56).

In words like young Wiglaf's, young Ælfwine called on the hard
core of the English at Maldon, when all that remained was to fight
on and die with their lord: 'Remember those times when often we
held forth at the mead-drinking, spoke vows aloud on the benches,
heroes in hall, concerning hard battle. Now he who is brave can
prove it.' And of the retainers of Hnaef the Half-Dane beleaguered
in a hall down in Frisia their poet says: 'I have never heard tell of
sixty victorious fighters bearing themselves better in heroic strife,
and never of young men better repaying the sweet (*or* white, i.e.
shining) mead than his warlike brood repaid Hnaef.' Gold, weapons,
mead are the recurring symbols of gift and payment, hospitality un-
stinted and service unto death, the full committal of lord to man and
man to lord.

Beowulf records many bounteous givings: arm-rings, torques,
weapons and armour, horses and harness, a tall standard with a
boar-image, publicly and honourably bestowed. And true it is, no
man can be mean and lordly both. It was Hrothgar's hope that he
might live in Heorot and share out among his retainers everything
which God had granted him, save the royal estates and the lives of
men. King Onela, the Scylfings' helm, was the best of sea-kings who
gave out rings in Sweden. Of Hygelac's power of giving we have
just spoken. The greater the king the more lavish his dispersals.
The generous gave for reward, in pay, to cement ties, from ostenta-
tion, and out of a generous heart. No Germanic, and for that matter
no Celtic, poet seems to have demurred.

Wisdom, in the formal statements of the heroic age, was an em-
bracing quality in which were subsumed education and training in
the young and a wealth of digested experience in the old, observa-
tion of events and the power to draw general conclusions from
them, insight into character and the ponderables of human nature,
and an unfailing awareness of the personal, social, and national (or
one might more safely say tribal) rights and duties, ties and accept-
ances, which alone made life meaningful and alone could make it
good. In *Beowulf* wisdom is the propriety of princes, their awareness

of justice, truth, and power, their distillation of the past, their insight into the future. That Hrothgar, an aged guardian of his people, should be wise is inevitable—the adjective *frōd* means both old and wise, as befits a patriarch—but wisdom is for the young too. Hrothgar has never heard a man so young as Beowulf discourse more wisely—surely the wise Lord himself had sent into his mind the words he uttered; and Hygd, the wife of Hygelac, though young, was wise and well accomplished. And if Hrothgar can make a shrewd cast into the future of the Geats, so can Beowulf into that of the Danes and Heathobards.

These virtues stand in *Beowulf* like four pillars in a royal hall. Kings are their surest possessors: Hrothgar, Hygelac, Beowulf himself, whose titles are not only *dryhten, frēa, cyning,* but *brytta,* breaker or dispenser (of gold), *helm,* helm or protector, *hyrde,* shepherd, keeper, guardian, *wine,* friend, and *wīsa,* leader, and many a compound, loving lord, gold-friend, gold-giver, army-leader, battle-leader, people's protector, war-king, and their like. But goodness is open to all, and without witness to the contrary is freely attributed. The presence of these unambiguous qualities, the unhedging praise they receive, and their working out in deed and ceremony, so warms and enriches the poem that the morality of *Beowulf* is as potent for the reader today as its wondertale narrative and heroic-historical trappings.

Finally (in this respect) we may note that just as the *Beowulf* poet thought fit to dress a tale of monsters in rich heroic raiment, so he rounded out the lean primary virtues with a Christian addendum, and on the whole did so with tact and sensitivity. The snarl of a zealot is completely absent, and rarely does he raise a castigatory finger. He approved of the men of old, and of antique virtue no less, and his indications of the superiority of his own Christian faith are by Christian standards almost ameliorative. The heathen, he recognized, had their problems.

That [Grendel's onset] was great sorrow and heartbreak to the Scyldings' friend. Many a lord sat ofttime in council, sought for a plan, what would be best for brave-hearted men to do in face of these sudden terrors. Sometimes they promised sacrifices at their heathen shrines, offered prayers that the destroyer of men's souls should provide help against the nation's disasters. Such was their practice, the hope of the heathen: their hearts were mindful of hell, but of the Creator they knew nothing, the judge of deeds; they had no knowledge of the Lord God; nor, truly, knew how to praise the Heavens' protector, the ruler of glory (170–83).[1]

He continues:

Woe shall it be for him who for dire enmity (*or* ill-will) shall thrust his soul down into the fire's embrace, expect no comfort, in any way to change. Well shall it be for him who after his deathday may meet with the Lord and seek peace in the Father's bosom (183–8).

Even so conventional a note as this is rarely sounded. What is more obvious, and certainly more important, is that Christianity serves a decisive function in refining and humanizing the poem's declared values. The groundwork of story is hard and violent; the legendary and historical additions are filled with war and feud; but Hrothgar and Beowulf are strongly attractive characters, the Dane benign and gracious, temperate and affectionate, the Geat all these things, modest and forbearing too. Both men are blessed with natural piety, practise truth and right among the people, and ponder the wisdom and mystery of Almighty God in his dealings with mankind. They are wholly free of that implacable heroic imbecility beloved of Saxo and the more strenuous Fornaldar Sögur. The tribute to Beowulf with which the poem ends is a Christian amelioration of the heroic ideal. 'Of all the kings of the world,' said the Geats, 'he was the mildest and gentlest of men, the kindest to his people, and the most eager for good report (*lofgeornost*).' The concluding adjective has begun to trouble subtle moralists, but that

---

[1] Much the same sentiment will be found in *King Hrolf's Saga*. 'The king's entire bodyguard had now fallen, so that no one of them survived, and most of the champions were mortally wounded, and this was the course of events which might be expected (said Master Galterus), that mortal strength might not withstand the strength of such fiends unless God's power should intervene —and that alone stood in the way of your victory, king Hrolf, that you knew naught of your Creator.' This relates to the last stand of Hrolf [the Hrothulf of *Beowulf*] and his champions at Lejre.

a hero should pursue *lof* and *dōm*, the good word of men in life and their earned commemoration after death, seems straightforward and laudable enough. For if this were vanity, as some mistakenly urge, it would be that precious refinement of it which all good men must possess if they are to strive not only for their own good name, a requisite of heroes both ancient and modern, but make a contribution to the general well-being. 'Cattle die, kinsmen die, the man himself must die. One thing I know that never dies: the good name of a man who dies.' These words belong to the cult of Odinn; the sentiment would be unexceptionable in any religion.

This is by no means the full spectrum of Christian colouring in *Beowulf*. But unless we accept quite unacceptable notions of the poem as a sustained, not to say unbroken and reinforced 'Allegory of Salvation', in which Beowulf's three wondertale exploits against Grendel, Grendel's Mother, and the Dragon are to be interpreted as aspects of the Redemption or reflections of New Testament narrative and theology (see p. 40 n., above), we find it remarkably free of specifically Christian dogma, as of formal Christian observance and ceremonial. There is a fair amount of Christian descriptive nomenclature, Father, Lord, Almighty, Creator, God, and an appreciable quantity of Old Testament reference (the Creation, Cain and Abel, Hell, the Deluge); God's will and governance are implicit throughout, but this is no more than the minimal and inevitable apparatus of an author raised in the Christian faith, versed in its primary documents, and given to improving discourse. Much more surprising is the circumstance that Christ is never mentioned, either as Son of Man or Son of God, and that no 'digression' (the brief and enigmatic reference to Hama seeking 'long-lasting gain', 1197–1201, carries little or no weight) has anything to say of Christian heroes, saints, disciples, or handmaidens of the Lord. Admittedly, if we see the Dragon (to press one analogy) as Satan, the faithless warband as the twelve apostles who betrayed the Son of Man into the hands of sinners, the unhappy fugitive who stole the Dragon's treasure-cup as Judas, and Wiglaf as a kind of John, the case is altered. If we go on to reject such other interpretations of the poem's narrative and substance as myth, wondertale, heroic legend, legendary history, and historical tradition severally and jointly provide—and

likewise discard the rival Christian interpretation of *Beowulf* as embodying the imperfect virtue of even virtuous heathendom or the
flawed state of the best of good men at all times and places—it is
altered still more. And if we can swallow not only the gnats of
allegory but the camels too—for example, the curious circumstance
that Christ's death saved mankind while Beowulf's ruined the Geats
—it is altered to the point of conviction. But these are vast triadic
ifs.

Blessedly, recognition of a consistent Christian colouring in
Beowulf does not depend on such far-reaching exegesis. The monsters
in human shape, Grendel in particular, are spoken of as hellish
creatures and enemies to God (*Godes ondsaca, fēond on helle, helrūnan,
helle hæfte*); and more is intended by this than our modern objurgations, 'fiend, devil, hell-hound', and the like. Grendel and his mother
are placed squarely with that foul brood of Cain who for a long and
horrid time fought against God and for that received their reward.
Grendel, specifically, bore the wrath of God (*Godes yrre bær*)—a
crushing phrase. So Beowulf has religion, justice, right, on his side
when he fights with him and his mother. In this, as we shall see
(pp. 82–3), he is a world apart from the heartless taskmen of *Culhwch
and Olwen*, and the Old English poem on a higher moral plane than
the Welsh narrative in prose. Even so it is hard to accept views of
Beowulf as an Old English *Gilgamesh*, the epic of a hero's battle
against the spiritual enemies of mankind, his early victories and
final defeat. Or an Old English *Völuspá* in which Beowulf-Thor
defends the divine Creation against its monstrous besiegers, and in
a minor Ragnarok encounters and is killed by Draca-Iormungandr;
for Beowulf is neither god nor god euhemerized, but man, hero,
mortal, and doomed by man's mortality not by Apocalypse. Nor is
it an Old English *Pilgrim's Progress*, save in so far as the life of any
good man exposed to the world's ills may be so regarded. Every man
born of woman is the unlit image of God, and every life a metaphor
of imperfection, but this makes neither myth nor allegory of *Beowulf*.
If in this we are right, or even approximately so, then the major
constituents of this unique and cherishable poem are not pagan or
Christian mythology, but heroic legend, wondertale, the dreams
and drowsings of pre-history, and an unremitting pre-occupation

with human values, as these are reflected in the best of pagan and Christian precept and example.

This still leaves us with something to say about *Beowulf* as heroic poetry and Beowulf as hero. Here as under other heads we are dealing with a complex and stratified composition.

A heroic poet is the accepted spokesman of a heroic society. A heroic poem is what he speaks on its behalf. It expresses the conventions, aspirations, and actions of such a society in the heightened and selective fashion characteristic of an artist. The two essential characteristics of such a society (we are concerned now only with the Indo-European family of peoples, from a literary point of view, and at a considerable distance in time) are that it shall be warlike and hierarchical, that is, controlled by a military aristocracy whose highest good is the warrior's code. 'War', says the *Bjarkamál*, 'springs from the nobly born. For the perilous deeds which leaders attempt are not to be done by the ventures of common men.' The three hundred heroes of the *Gododdin* were three hundred chieftains: for the bard the rank and file accompanying them did not count, and were not counted. But for a lord:

Isag the distinguished man from the region of the South, his manners were like the sea-flood for graciousness and liberality and pleasant mead-drinking. Where his weapons gouged requital was abandoned. His sword echoed in the heads of mothers; the rampart of fury, he was renowned, the son of Gwyddnau (A.27).

Fighting was a free man's business, his pleasure and his duty. This is the witness of Tacitus respecting the Germans in the first century A.D., and of Strabo and Posidonius respecting the Celts a hundred years earlier. If there is a straw's width between them, it is that Tacitus says that among the Germans the leader fights for victory and his followers fight for the leader, whereas classical witness to the Celts records that they will fight anyone, anytime, anywhere, for any reason, or for no reason at all. Human nature changes little, and it may well be that in any more sublimated sense than this a Heroic Age is merely our modern endorsement of the cherished illusion of a self-regarding ruling caste and its creative artists. The reality, no doubt, if we were acquainted with it, would show more squalid than fine, more brutal than brave, a smirched ornament on a dunghill of human misery and oppression.[1] Even so, nothing in our lives is more powerful than our illusions, and nothing more shapes our art. We know precisely where we are, and what we are dealing with, when we hear poetry like this:

Wearing a brooch, in the front rank, armed in the battle-shout, a mighty man in combat before his deathday, a leader charging for-wards before armies. There fell five times fifty before his blades; of the men of Deira and Bernicia there fell a hundred score; they were annihilated in one hour. He would sooner be meat for wolves than go to a wedding, he would sooner be prey for the raven than go to the altar, he would sooner his blood flowed to the ground than that he should get due burial, in return for mead in the hall among the hosts. Hyfaidd the Tall shall be honoured as long as there is a minstrel (A.5).

Or this:

Sweet is it to repay the gifts received from our lord, to grip the swords, and devote the steel to glory. Behold, each man's courage tells him loyally to follow a king of such deserts, and to guard our captain with fitting earnestness. Let the Teuton swords, the helmets, the shining armlets, the mailcoats that reach the heel, which Hrolf of old bestowed upon his men, let these sharpen our mindful hearts to the fray. The time requires, and it is just, that in time of war we should earn whatsoever we have gotten in the deep idleness of peace . . . My master is the greatest of the Danes: let each man, as he is valorous, stand by him; far, far hence be all cowards!

Or yet again, this:

Byrhtwold spoke, raised his shield on high; he was a liegeman of long standing, brandished his ash-spear, full bravely he exhorted the

[1] I know of nowhere where the issues are more sharply presented in a modern context than in T. E. Lawrence, *Seven Pillars of Wisdom* (1935), chapter CXVII, the affair at Tafas.

warriors. 'Thought shall be harder, heart the keener, courage the greater, as our might lessens. Here lies our lord all hewn down, a good man in the dust. Ever may he feel sorrow who thinks now to turn from this war-play. I am old in years, and will not leave this place. I reckon to lie at my lord's side, that man so dear to me.

War, valour, service, loyalty, liberality, contempt of death, and love of fame: these are the constants of truly heroic verse. The more a poem confines itself to such basic assumptions as an unbreakable bond between lord and liegeman, an acknowledged pattern of duty and reward, open-handedness in peace and ferocity in combat, a love of fame and horror of disgrace; the more resolutely it avoids all such contaminatory themes as love, treasure, profit, revenge, jealousy, patriotism, religion, the rational or the supernatural, and holds to the exertion of the warrior's will in the starkest and most inescapable situation; the more purely heroic it will be. Three such have been quoted from above: the Welsh *Gododdin*, the Norse *Bjarkamál*, the English *Battle of Maldon*. All three are heroic poems in a sense in which *Beowulf* is not. All three accept the heroic ethos without question or debate. All three are exalted utterances telling of a man's duty to his lord and of the excellence of that lord. All three deal with a single situation, whose disaster is its glory, and whose glory its disaster. All three are about men in a narrow place, the defence of a causeway (*Maldon*), the assault on a strong position (the *Gododdin*), the beleaguering of a royal residence (*Bjarkamál*), where the bodyguard cannot go forward and will not go back, but will die for its lord where it stands, and chooses so to die. All three in their intention, though not in their manner, are simple and straightforward, poems of absolute commitment. The *Gododdin*, indeed, may well be the poem which most closely conforms among all the literatures of the Germanic and Celtic peoples to the heroic ideal and its severest conventions. Even a brief account of it allows us to see how different in kind it is from *Beowulf*, and how much more and, one thinks, how much better than a heroic poem *Beowulf* is.

The *Gododdin*, reputedly composed by the poet Aneirin not long after the battle of which it tells, has been ascribed, convincingly but

not unanimously, to *c.* 600.[1] Early Welsh literature has many heroic
or heroic-elegiac poems but no epic, or even sustained narrative,
because the bards, or poets, did not practise a long sustained mode
of composition, beginning more or less at the beginning, and
proceeding more or less tidily to a more or less defined end. They
were less narrators than celebrants: the 'story' so to speak was
known, and assumed to be known: the last thing the poet of the
Gododdin proposed to do was tell us what happened. His intention
was to commemorate the heroes who fell at Catraeth. What happened at Catraeth has to emerge, be pieced together, from his series
of elegies and panegyrics. It may be a simplification to say of the
Celtic Heroic Age in Britain, as this is recorded in its verse, that the
warrior lived that he might be glorified by the bard, and the bard
lived that he might glorify the warrior, but it is a simplification
free from distortion. *Beird byt barnant wyr o galon*: 'The poets of the
world pass judgement on men of valour'. Which our poet does
pre-eminently. 'He slew a great host to win reputation; the son of
Nwython slew a hundred gold-torqued princes that he might win
praise.' 'Sywno's son (the soothsayer knew it) sold his life for the
mention of glory.' 'It would be wrong to leave him unremembered
. . . most hostile in battle, the generous wyvern, dragon in blood-
shed after the wine-feast, Gwenabwy son of Gwen, in the conflict
at Catraeth.' 'Famed son of Clydno, I shall sing to you, lord, praise
without end, without limit.' And of the three hundred who rode
out and died the poet sings: 'Three hundred gold-torqued men
made the attack, defended their land, with cruel slaughter. Al-
though they were slain, they slew, and till the end of the world they
shall be praised.' Each verse of the *Gododdin* commemorates the army
of Mynyddog or one or more of its members; the political, dynastic,

---

[1] The poem is preserved in the so-called Book of Aneirin in the Cardiff Free
Library, in two versions: Version A (88 stanzas) written in the orthography
of the thirteenth century; Version B (42 stanzas) in the orthography of the
ninth or tenth. It has been edited by Sir Ifor Williams, *Canu Aneirin*, Cardiff,
1938; translated into English prose with a substantial apparatus in English
by Professor Kenneth Jackson, *The Gododdin*, Edinburgh, 1969; and discussed
in the context of 'The heroic ideal in early Welsh poetry' in a paper under that
name by Professor A. O. H. Jarman (*Beiträge zur Indogermanistik und Keltologie;
Julius Pokorny zum 80. Geburtstag gewidmet*, herausgegeben von Wolfgang
Meid, Innsbruck, 1967, pp. 193–211).

strategic background of the action, and much of the action itself, must be inferred.

That action was an attack near the year 600 upon the English of Deira and Bernicia, the future kingdom of Northumbria, mounted by Mynyddog, the British king of the North British people and land known as Gododdin. To this end he collected fighting-men from all the British realms and feasted them for a year before the attack took place. 'Wine and mead from golden vessels were their drink for a year, by noble custom.' And as they feasted, wine-feast and mead-feast, 'great was their planning and boasting.' At the year's end they took their weapons and mounted their swan-hued, shaggy-maned horses. Their line of advance was from Edinburgh (Din Eidyn) to Catterick (Catraeth) in northern Yorkshire. At Catraeth the Three Hundred encountered the hosts of England (Lloegr) and were annihilated save for one man—or maybe three. Like the flower of the Danes and Geats in *Beowulf*, the retainers of Hnaef the Half-Dane down in Frisia, king Hrolf's champions at Lejre, and Byrhtnoth's proud thanes at Maldon, they made payment for their mead (*talu medd*) with their lives. 'The men went to Catraeth, swift was their host; the pale mead was their feast and it was their poison. Three hundred fighting according to plan, and after the jubilation there was silence' (A.8).

The *Gododdin* inevitably has some things in common with *Beowulf*, but in various striking ways they are far apart. *Beowulf* is a long poem, of more than three thousand lines, divisible at most into two parts. The *Gododdin* runs to more than twelve hundred lines, and even when we excise the readily recognized interpolations and repetitions we are left with a thousand. But these are not disposed after the fashion of *Beowulf* in narrative order, but may well be regarded as roughly a hundred short poems bound together by a common occasion and purpose. It is obviously much easier to maintain purity of mood, and still more a limitation of mood, in short poems than in a long. As we have seen, in a poem as long and leisurely as *Beowulf* other things keep pushing in: sentiment, philosophy, morals, religion, history, statecraft, reflection, even a sense of the future. The Britons of the *Gododdin* are Christians, and the English are referred to contemptuously as heathens; but the

7. ARMED MAN BETWEEN BEASTS
From Torslunda

values of the poem, in contrast to those of *Beowulf*, show no Christian amelioration; there are few references to Christian practice; and
God goes unmentioned.

Not only the *Beowulf* poet's insistence on wisdom and piety, the
homiletic, moralizing, and reflective cast of his mind, but his compassion and tolerance are against him as an archetypal heroic poet.
When Hnaef and his Half-Danes are trapped in a hall down in
Frisia, and when Hengest avenges his dead lord on Finn, what our
poet feels (in contrast to the author of the exultant 'Finnesburg
Fragment') is not only the inevitability of the action but the grief
and pain of it. Helpless between these grim men stands the Danish
princess Hildeburh, and our poet sees that whoever gains she must
lose. Her husband and sons will be killed on one side, and her
brother and fellow-countrymen on the other. *Þæt wæs geōmuru ides*:
'That was an unhappy lady!' But in the *Gododdin* grief was felt only
for one's own.

> The warriors rose up, mustered together, with one accord they
> attacked; short were their lives, long the grief for them among their
> kinsmen. They slew seven times their number of English. In war they
> made women widows, many a mother with tears on her eyelids (A.56).

The conclusion of this summary stanza, like the shattering line
quoted earlier in the panegyric on Isag (p. 50), *Seinnyessyt e gledyf
ym penn mameu*: 'His sword echoed in the heads of mothers!', shows
neither pity nor contrition. It is boasting and exultation. A century
of such stanzas, lyrical, elegiac, and celebratory, occasionally strung
together by the repetition or near-repetition of a first line, but for
the most part not markedly consecutive, but rather swinging out
from then closing back on a central theme of devotion, death, and
glory, so that the poem's chronology exists in the mind not con-
secutively but simultaneously, and its theme and action grow from
the unremitting to the obsessive—these constitute, surely, the
most whole-hearted exposition of the heroic ideal in western
literature. Alongside it *Maldon* and *Beowulf* are very English, not
only in their language and the unexcessive treatment of their
subjects, but in their fidelity to what the English still like to consider

8. ARMED MAN BETWEEN DRAGONLIKE BEASTS
He has thrust his sword (mid-right) through one, whose head lies left
of bottom centre, and the other is inflicting a fearsome wound on his
throat. From Tyldal.

their instinctive (and cultivated) virtues in times of trial: calm fortitude, devotion to duty, and bravery without histrionics.

But by now there is no need to recapitulate the many-sided excellences of *Beowulf*, or illustrate anew its broad humanity. It will be more useful to amplify our view of how well its poet has done. Its contents make it important to students of many disciplines and literatures, but in themselves are no guarantee of literary merit. What more may be said, briefly and finally, of the poem's quality?

Our author's most apparent poetic gift is his unflurried professional competence. We may begin by accepting that he knew what he was doing. Even in the so-called digressions he had a purpose, though at times we are less convinced than he of its validity, and once he is over his transition we find he always has good words, command of metre, an assured manner, and a mastery of mood. It is a primary virtue in an extended poem to keep it moving, which he does. And at its proper pace, which he does. Its leisureliness rests on strength, its ruminations, such as Hrothgar's homily, the passage devoted to the lone survivor's burial of a people's treasure, and the misery of the father bereft of his hanged son, are the unforced expression of matters dear to the poet's heart. It would be special pleading to call *Beowulf* wisdom literature, but its action is weighted with sentiments concerning virtue, life, and destiny, couched in words that convince and verse that sustains. Its author had a good eye and ear, a well-stored mind, and high expertise in verse-making. He had at command the full professional vocabulary of the Old English poet, both that abundance of synonyms and near-synonyms without which alliterative verse cannot prosper (and without which he would have been denied a sometimes conventional but frequently telling choice of names for, let us say, man, sea, ship, sword, and ruler[1]) and that apparatus of metaphor and kenning which at its freshest gives tang and savour in almost any context: swan-road, whale-road, sail-road (sea), battle-light (sword), bone-house (body), heaven's jewel, world-candle (sun). He was a skilful manipulator of the meaningful variation of phrase, clause, or expression which is a major feature of the Old English poetic

[1] For *king*-words, see p. 46.

repertoire; the whole craft of alliterative verse was familiar to him, its devices and techniques, and he used it with a manly but unforced authority. This, and what may be called his holding quality as a narrator, observer of scenes and manners, and ponderer of human affairs must now be a shade unsatisfactorily illustrated through the medium of translation. Here is his account of Beowulf's sea-voyage from the country of the Geats to Heorot:

Time wore on. The ship was on the waves, the boat under the lee of the cliff. The warriors, all ready, went up on board at the prow. Currents eddied, the sea upon the shore; men carried their glittering array, their noble war-gear, into the bosom of the ship; heroes thrust out the well-braced vessel on their welcome adventure. Impelled by the wind, the foamy-necked wave-floater sped over the billowy sea, most like to a bird, until about the due time the next day its curved prow had made such a journey that the sailors saw land, sea-cliffs shining, tall hills and broad sea-nesses. The sea was traversed and their voyage at an end. The Weders went up on shore, secured their vessel, their sarks and armour rang. They gave thanks to God that their passage had been easy (210–28).

Here is his most famous piece of emotively descriptive writing, with its reminiscences of Virgil and the 17th Blickling Homily, the desolate vagueness of its landscape, the disturbing quality of its animal vignette:

They dwell in a secret place, wolf-slopes, windy nesses, perilous paths through the fens, where the mountain-stream goes down under the mists of the cliffs, the flood below ground. It is not far hence in miles that that mere will be found. Frosty groves hang over it, whose trees, firm-rooted, canopy the water. There may be seen each night a fearful wonder—flame on the face of the pool. No man lives so old and wise that he knows what lies down under. Though the strong-horned hart, the heath-ranger, should make for that wood, hard-pressed by hounds and hunted from afar, he will sooner give up his life and being on its brink than plunge in to hide his head. It is not a wholesome place. From its surface, when the wind stirs up hateful storms, the dark tormented water swirls up to meet the clouds, till the air fills with mist, the heavens weep (1357–76).

Though trenchant at times in his major transitions, he can be deft at the heroic parenthesis. As part of his reward for killing Grendel, Beowulf has just received from Wealhtheow's hand 'the greatest of neck-rings I have ever heard tell of on earth.' The poet continues:

That neck-ring Hygelac of the Geats, Sverting's grandson, had with him on his last expedition, when he defended his treasure under his banner, guarded his warspoils. Fate carried him off when he recklessly courted disaster, feud with the Frisians. The mighty lord wore that ornament, those precious stones, over the waves' bowl: he perished under his shield. The king's body fell then into the hands of the Franks, his armour, and the torque with it. Warriors less worthy plundered the slain after the carnage; the Geat folk held the field of slaughter (1202–14).

This is noble. Hygelac is a doer, and doers, we know, must suffer. His valour, pride, daring, and bad luck escorted him, almost formally, with ships and brave array to his bloody death at the hands of the Franks in Frisia. His men died with him. They held the place of slaughter because in battle they would not, and after battle could not, quit it.

He can always move us with a rumination of age and mortality, life's waning and the certitude of sorrow. An old man, the sorely tried Hrothgar, is speaking:

Guard yourself, dear Beowulf, best of men, against such wicked anger; choose the better part, eternal gain. Keep yourself from pride, famed warrior. Now is the flower of your might but for a while; soon it shall happen that sickness or the sword will part you from your strength, or the embrace of fire, or the welling of a flood, blade's onset or the flight of a spear, or terrible old age; or your eyes' brightness shall fail and grow dim. Presently it must happen that death will overcome you, warrior! (1758–68).

And finally, at the poem's end, when all must be true and fine, and one false word or forced sentiment would jar unbearably, he rises to his task with dignity and power. In forty-five lines he rounds off his narrative, describes his hero's obsequies and the grief of his people, and brings all to a close with a eulogy as noble and a cadence as conclusive as any in medieval literature:

Then the Geat people prepared for him on that ground a firm-based funeral pyre, hung about with helms and warshields and glittering corslets, even as he had requested. Heroes lamenting laid in its midst the famous prince, their beloved lord. Then the warriors began to kindle the greatest of funeral fires on the mound. The dark wood-smoke clambered high over the burning, the flame's roaring mingled with the sound of tears, the wind's tumult grew still, till it had crumbled the bones' frame, hot to its core. With grieving hearts they proclaimed their misery, the killing of their lord. Further, the sad lady of the Geats, her hair bound back, sang in a sorrowful chant that she greatly feared mournful days, dread of foes, oppression and captivity. Heaven swallowed up the smoke.

Then the Weder folk raised a shelter on the headland which was tall and broad and visible from afar to voyagers over the sea; and in ten days they built a memorial to the brave warrior. They constructed a wall around what the fire had left, even as the wisest of men might most honourably devise it. They placed in the barrow circlets and jewels, all such adornments as warlike men had earlier taken from the hoard; let the earth keep the treasures of heroes, gold in the ground, where it still abides, as useless to men as it was in the beginning.

Men brave in battle, sons of princes, twelve in number rode round the mound. They wished to proclaim their grief, mourn for their king, utter a dirge, and tell about the man. They exalted his high worth, extolled his valiant deeds, even as it is fitting that men should praise their beloved lord in words, and cherish him at heart when he must be led forth from his earthly body.

So the Geat people, his hearth-comrades, sorrowed after the fall of their lord; said that of all the kings of the world he was the mildest and gentlest of men, the kindest to his people, and the most eager for good fame (3137–82).

This then is our poem, which can be approached in many ways and admired for many reasons. Because it is unique, and because of its great assurance, and not least because of its story-telling, we may not improperly be tempted to prize it too highly, and grow recondite in its justification. There may, we are reminded, have been better poems written by better poets in the eighth and early ninth centuries even as there were brave men before Agamemnon. But this is a large assumption, and if there were they are perished, as though they had never been. But *Beowulf* we have, with its admirable two parts of story, its embellishments from Germanic tradition and its glimpses of early history, its patterns of excellence to imitate, its models of evil to be declined. It is concerned to teach, and acquaints us with virtue, would make us better men. And why not? No one in his right mind thinks that poetry, or any art, should make us worse. For all its monsters it portrays a warm and human world, and does it with a hundred happy touches: feasting in hall, voyaging by sea and riding afield; courteous greetings and sad farewells; the bestowing of gifts and pledging of friendship. A king sits on his throne, wise, valiant and generous; a ring-adorned queen moves through the hall, and from her jewelled hand warriors accept the brimming mead-cup; on the cliff-edge a sentinel stares out to sea, watchful for friend and foe alike; an embittered veteran broods on ancient wrongs and present revenge; a bride, young and necklaced, walks into hall on the arm of her belted escort.[1] In no poem are we more aware of convention, and in few do we so readily accept it. Joy and sorrow are the common lot, and, under heaven, men must

[1] Some of these are stereotypes: a king, queen, or warrior is observed typically, in his public image and occupation. When Beowulf and his companions return to the land of the Geats they proceed quickly 'to where as they heard tell the protector of warriors, that good young war-king the slayer of Ongentheow, was distributing rings inside the stronghold' (1964-70). At the beer-drinking in Heorot, Wealhtheow, Hrothgar's queen, 'came forth, mindful of her role; gold-adorned she greeted the men in hall . . . the lady of the Helmings went round the warriors, the tried men and the youths, bore them the mead-cup' (612-24). Before the dragon-fight the prince of the Weder-Geats, 'because he was enraged (*gebolgen*, swollen, physically dilated with rage: the poem is full of these powerful physical images which tend to be enfeebled in translation), let a shout come forth from his breast, stark-hearted he stormed, his voice came echoing in, a clear challenge to battle under the grey rock' (2550-53). The effect is noble and formal, fixing the subject as though in tapestry. The poet is particularly successful in his portraiture of the Danish royal house: the aged white-haired king, his handsome, active, gracious consort, their sacrificial daughter, and their negligible young sons, all with the aspect and posture suited to their role in the poem and tradition.

make of their lives what they can. For they enjoy the light and warmth and company in hall but for a while, and outside is the encompassing dark. 'Presently it must happen that death will overcome you, warrior.' On earth there will remain the good name of a good man; beyond earth a refuge in the Father's arms. It is satisfactory to be assured that this fierce and gentle warrior, Beowulf of the Geats, found both.

II. CULHWCH AND OLWEN

1. Hero with Helpers

CULHWCH AND OLWEN (*CULHWCH AC OLWEN*) IS PART of the *Mabinogion*, and it is by way of the *Mabinogion* that most of its readers approach it. It is by way of the *Mabinogion* we approach it in our turn.

The *Mabinogion* is the title, or happy misnomer, bestowed in the nineteenth century on eleven medieval prose stories preserved in two Welsh collections, the White Book of Rhydderch (*Llyfr Gwyn Rhydderch*), which was written down about 1300–25 and is now preserved in the National Library of Wales, and the Red Book of Hergest (*Llyfr Coch Hergest*), of the period 1375–1425, now in the possession of Jesus College, Oxford. In the White Book *Culhwch and Olwen* will be found only in part; and it is the Red Book which preserves what in the absence of any other manuscript authority we must regard as the story in its entirety. The eleven stories of the *Mabinogion* fall into three easily distinguishable and yet interrelated groups. First there are the Four Branches of the Mabinogi, *Pwyll Prince of Dyfed*, *Branwen Daughter of Llŷr*, *Manawydan Son of Llŷr*, and *Math Son of Mathonwy*, four reworkings of Celtic or indeed more universal story material, as architecturally disjointed and confused in their matter as they are exquisite in style and enchanting in their episodes. They appear to be the work of one author. Second come four native tales independent of the Four Branches on the one hand and of the Romances on the other—and, unlike the Four Branches, independent of each other. Two of them are short wonder-tales, entitled *The Dream of Macsen Wledig* and *The Adventure of Lludd and Llefelys*. The other two, *Culhwch and Olwen* and *The Dream of Rhonabwy*, are in their different ways extended and elaborate compositions, the first excelling in the force and variety of its high-paced deployment of story, the second in the brilliance and intricacy of its descriptive set-pieces. Not that *Culhwch* is without description or *Rhonabwy* without a story: colourful action and a sense of style are two of the more immediately apparent characteristics of all *Mabinogion* stories. Both *Culhwch* and *Rhonabwy* have much to tell of Arthur and his warriors; but even so their 'British' provenance sets them emphatically apart from the three so-called 'French' Arthurian romances of the third group: *The Lady of the Fountain, Peredur son of Efrawg,* and *Gereint son of Erbin.* It is generally held that the writing down of the Four Branches in the form in which we have them, as distinct from their copying into the White Book and the Red, may be ascribed to the third quarter of the eleventh century. The decisive redaction of *Culhwch and Olwen* must be set as far back as the year 1100, and maybe half a century earlier. Its subject-matter, like that of the Four Branches and the other native tales (and substantial portions of the three Arthurian romances), goes back farther still, some of it to the dawn of story-telling in Asia and Europe.

Every reader of the eleven stories of the *Mabinogion* is quickly aware of marked differences in their substance, manner, tone, atmosphere, and degree of antiquity. They range from the primitive to the courtly, the heroic to the romantic, the charming to the terrible, the fantastic to the matter-of-fact; from comedy to tragedy, the pathetic to the sublime; from a harsh simplicity to a refined sophistication. The *Mabinogion* is at once a book and a library. Even so, the stories are bound together by ties more compelling than their preservation in the same manuscripts. For one thing they are all Welsh and display, or remember, common habits of narration. For another, despite their variety they belong to a common literary and social setting. And third, there is a linking thread in their subject matter. The story-tellers of the *Mabinogion* are to a high degree reworkers of older material, borrowers from an often remote antiquity, the inheritors of themes and stories whose significance has begun to escape them.

What was the nature and substance of this material? Was it anything that can legitimately be called history? The answer is assuredly No. The kings and princes of the Four Branches, whatever their announced dominion, are not historical personages. Yet persons known to history there certainly are: Taliesin the sixth-century poet for one (he is named in *Culhwch and Olwen*), and Caswallon, who was known to Julius Caesar as Cassivelaunus, for another (he is named in the Second Branch). Macsen, in the story which bears his name, was the Spanish-born Magnus Maximus who invaded Gaul in the year 383 and was killed at Aquileia five years later; and the hero of one of the romances, *The Lady of the Fountain*, who also plays a belligerent and puzzling role in *The Dream of Rhonabwy*, is Owein son of Urien, a famed prince of the North Britons in the late sixth century. And there is Arthur himself, much to the fore in both *Culhwch and Olwen* and *The Dream*, as well as in the Romances proper. But in the *Mabinogion* these do not play a historical role. Rather, they are half-remembered figures from a misty past, grown increasingly wondrous and larger than life, and attracting to themselves or being otherwise involved with the folk literature of earlier centuries, to which the word 'historical' cannot be applied.

If not history, is the subject matter of the *Mabinogion* myth in decline? If so, the decline has gone a long way, and the modern decline in belief in a mythological background or underswell for the stories and persons of the *Mabinogion* still farther. Admittedly the Four Branches and *Culhwch and Olwen* preserve the names of a few ancient Celtic gods and goddesses, like the children of Dôn and the children of Llŷr, Lleu (here Lleu Llaw Gyffes, i.e. Lleu of the Deft Hand, in the Fourth Branch reduced to the offspring of a magician and a king's footholder, but no god), and Mabon son of Modron, of whom we shall have reason to speak later (p. 84ff). But that process of speculation characteristic of the nineteenth century, which saw everywhere in early Celtic and Teutonic literature sky-gods, sun-gods, weather-gods, vegetation-gods, and the hypothetical beliefs and presumed narrative explanations associated with these in the rather facilely reconstructed Indo-European mind, has fallen (maybe too far) into disrepute.[1]

[1] 'These scattered appearances of purely Celtic divine figures and possible exiguous fragments of their myth are inheritances from the pagan Celtic period which were used by the original composers of the first tales, and round them there has been assembled a mass of popular-tale motifs of very varied

Above all the Four Branches and *Culhwch and Olwen* are re-tellings of international or Celtic wondertale and other traditional folk-literature. There is no question of their being put together as a historical record; and they are not interpretable in a systematized or even coherent fashion as portrayals or illuminations of myths. *Culhwch and Olwen* displays a most elaborate pattern of plots and motifs, many of them known in many lands over many centuries, others possibly of native provenance. Among the more traceable incorporated or adapted stories are Six go through the World, the Magic Flight, the Grateful Animals, the Oldest on the Farm, the Man on the Quest of his Lost Wife, the Oldest Animals (which exists in Welsh independently of *Culhwch and Olwen*), and the Search for the Prisoner. In addition there is the well-developed story of the Hunting of Twrch Trwyth, that of the Unending Battle, and a score or more indications of stories, motifs, themes in our author's account of the warriors at Arthur's court and the list of marvellous things demanded by Ysbaddaden towards the Winning of the Giant's Daughter. Of these last two categories some we know of, some we can guess at, but of others we may well remain ignorant for ever.

We are now, perhaps, in a position to ask ourselves the key questions: What is *Culhwch and Olwen*? And what is it about? Primarily it is the re-telling of a widely dispersed and long-flourishing wondertale. It is Culhwch's destiny that he shall marry none save Olwen, daughter of Ysbaddaden Chief Giant; with the aid of Arthur and his men he finds his bride, accomplishes the tasks her father sets him, and marries her.

If we generalize the story, so that we employ no proper names but instead indicate its protagonists, it can be described thus: A

origin, international and non-international, just as King Arthur is a figure of early history round whom gathered a quantity of exactly the same kind of thing. By and large, however, I think it is wise to regard mythological explanations of even the non-international episodes in the *Mabinogion* with a cautious scepticism. . . . In any case, no theory involving the supposition of a myth should even be advanced until one has made sure that the motif one is studying is not an international one.' Kenneth Hurlstone Jackson, *The International Popular Tale and Early Welsh Tradition*, Cardiff, 1961, p. 129. For an elaborate re-statement, in the light of early religion and anthropology, of the mythological and traditional bases of Irish and Welsh story see Alwyn Rees and Brinley Rees, *Celtic Heritage*, 1961.

hero wishes to marry a giant's daughter, an undertaking which has so far proved fatal to all who have attempted it. With the help of men of extraordinary powers he reaches the giant's house, meets the giant's daughter, who counsels him how he may win her. The giant demands the performance of various seemingly impossible tasks as the price of his consent. With the help of the wondrous companions these are achieved, the giant is put to death, and the hero marries the daughter.

This is the wondertale known to the classifiers of folktale as 'Six go through the (whole) World' (Aarne–Thompson 513A, 513), but to a host of less professional readers as 'How the Hero won the Giant's Daughter'. Here is the A–T analysis of Type 513, 'The Helpers', which takes in 513A, 'Six go through the World', as its sections II and III.

I. *The Hero.* (a) The hero unlike his elder brothers has been kind to an old man (*b*) *who helps him provide* a ship that goes both on land and water (*c*) *for the building of which the king will give his daughter in marriage.*—(d) The hero is aided by a grateful dead man.
II. *The Companions. The hero is joined one after the other by extraordinary companions:* (a) a man so strong that he pulls up trees, (*b*) *one who shoots the left eye of a fly at two miles' distance,* (c) a great blower, (*d*) *a great hearer,* (*e*) *a great runner,* (*f*) *a withstander of cold,* (*g*) *etc.*
III. *Help of the Companions. They help the hero* (a) defeat the princess in a race for her hand, (*b*) *perform tasks set by the king or enchantress:* (*c*) *eating,* (*d*) *drinking,* (*e*) *withstanding cold,* (*f*) *carrying off money,* (g) bringing a ring from the sea, (h) guarding a maiden, (i) bringing a maiden, (*j*) *bringing a magic remedy,* (*k*) *annihilating a pursuing army,* etc.[1]

---

[1] As for *Beowulf* above (pp. 8–10) I transcribe the A–T list of motifs, with their references to the Stith Thompson *Motif-Index.* The italics here and in the analysis above are my own.
I. Q2. Kind and unkind. L13. Compassionate youngest son. N825.2. Help from old man. D1533.1.1. Magic land and water ship. H335. *Tasks assigned suitors. Bride as prize for accomplishment.* H331. Suitor contest: bride offered as prize. H972. Tasks accomplished with help of grateful dead.
II. F601. Extraordinary companions. *A group of strong men with extraordinary powers travel together.* F621. Strong man: tree-puller. Can uproot all trees. F622. Mighty blower. Man turns mill with his blowing. *F661.5.3. Skillful marksman shoots left eye of fly at two miles.* G641.1. Man can hear grass (wool) grow. *F.641.2. Man can hear ant leave nest fifty miles away.* F641.3. Man can hear

With this in mind, we may now expand our one-sentence summary of *Culhwch and Olwen*, and so learn something of our author's management of his story-material. Culhwch is the son of Cilydd by his first wife Goleuddydd. His destiny in respect of Olwen is laid on him by Cilydd's second wife, because he will not marry her daughter by her own first marriage. The issue is put earthily: 'Thy side shall never knock against woman till thou win Olwen daughter of Ysbaddaden Chief Giant.' On his father's advice Culhwch proceeds to his kinsman Arthur's court and invokes a boon in the name of Arthur's warriors and the gold-torqued maidens of this Island. Arthur grants the boon, but for a whole year the maiden cannot be found, till Culhwch sets forth with six of Arthur's men and comes at last to the greatest of forts in the world. With the connivance of the shepherd Custennin and his wife, twenty-three of whose sons Ysbaddaden Chief Giant has slain, they speak with Olwen, and thereafter have three savagely grotesque interviews with Ysbaddaden himself. The giant recounts some two-score tasks which must be fulfilled before Culhwch shall have his daughter. We hear of the accomplishment of roughly one-third of these, and there is a general statement that they have all been accomplished. Those described include, or involve, the Grateful Animals, the Search for

---

one sleeping by putting ear to ground. *F681.1. Marvellous runner* keeps leg tied up. To prevent him from running away. *F685. Marvellous withstander of cold. F633. Mighty drinker. Drinks up whole pool of water, or the like. F632. Mighty eater. Eats whole ox at a time, or the like.* D2144.1.2. Man with power to make everything freeze wears cap over his ear to prevent this.

III. F601.2. Extraordinary companions help hero in suitor tests. H331.5.1. Race with princess for her hand. *F601.1. Extraordinary companions perform hero's tasks.* H1450.1. Waking contest. H1114. Task: eating enormous amount. H1142. Task: drinking enormous amount. H1512. Cold test. Attempt to freeze hero to death. H1511. Heat test. Attempt to kill hero by burning him in fire. H1127. Task: carrying off huge quantity of money. H1132.1. Task: recovering lost objects from sea. H1324. Quest for marvellous remedy. D1240. Magic waters and medicines. H1135. Task: annihilating (overcoming) army single-handed. L161. Lowly *hero marries princess.*

One could well italicize all the tasks in III. Named members of Arthur's court show that their undertakers were ready at hand; but in the event the thirty-nine named tasks show differences from those listed for A–T 513, in part because of the Celtic setting.

Much of II and III, both analysis and motifs, will be found relevant to *King Hrolf's Saga* (see in particular pp. 144–6 below).

9. A WELSH WARRIOR
From Eglwysilan

the Prisoner, the Oldest Animals, the Unending Battle, and the Hunting of the Boar, Twrch Trwyth, in which Arthur and his hosts play a prominent part. The tasks completed, Culhwch sets forth with Goreu son of Custennin (the twenty-fourth and only surviving son: his name means Best); the giant is shaved and slain. 'And that night Culhwch slept with Olwen, and she was his only wife so long as he lived. And the hosts of Arthur dispersed, every one to his country. And in this wise did Culhwch win Olwen, daughter of Ysbaddaden Chief Giant.'

These are still the big bones rather than the fully articulated skeleton, to say nothing of the flesh and fell, of *Culhwch and Olwen*. But for the moment they will serve. Obviously the story of 'Six go through the World', as it reached these Islands, has been extensively worked up through the addition of other popular tales (two of them, and as it happens the best of them, arguably developed at disproportionate length), and it has been attached to the native British tradition of Arthur, hero and folk-leader. What results is a storehouse of folktale and a window upon legend; a Celtic thesaurus, and at the same time the first sustained prose narrative to tell of our British Arthur in the literature of Europe; a series of striking vignettes and powerfully executed episodes; a vigorous display of a vigorous style applied to vigorous subject matter; and, not least, a splendid if somewhat disorderly narrative.

Of its author, that impressive, irregular artist of the tenth or eleventh century, to whom, in accordance with convention, we assign the honour of a final redaction of the story-material, we know nothing. His name, fortune, and life's course are all hidden from us. But he was clearly a man of tremendous and distinctive literary gifts, with a virtuoso's joy in their employment. Language for him was an instrument of effect, and preferably rhetorical effect. Always he wrote out of power and zest, now with a brutal curtness, now with a cool lyricism; he is as successful with the gravely beautiful as with the headlong gasconade. He is for ever startling us with some new resource of style; we share his excitement at what he is doing and what he may do next. His especial forte is for the grotesque and a nonchalant ferocity. By design (or some subsequent maiming—which seems unlikely) he is an early master of the absurd.

10. THE GUNDESTRUP CAULDRON
Celtic gods and goddesses with animal and human figures. *Centre top:* a procession of helmeted foot soldiers, horsemen, and horn-blowers.

He has a power of suggestion at once exhilarating and disturbing. Eye-widening fantasy or hair-raising craziness invariably kindle him to brave performance. His sentences never trickle: they jet under pressure. Yet though exultant and exuberant, he is not undisciplined. His surging power is harnessed to an artistic purpose, and he is sworn foe of the unnecessary word.

The bite of his speech and the brevity of his expression are as remarkable as the extravagance of his fancy. Witness his cameos. Morfran son of Tegid: 'No man placed his weapon in him at Camlan, so exceeding ugly was he; all thought he was a devil helping. There was hair on him like the hair of a stag.' Sandde Angel-face: 'No one placed his spear in him at Camlan, so exceeding fair was he; all thought he was an angel helping.' Or Cynyr Fair-beard and his refrigerative sentence to his wife about their son Cei: 'If there be anything of me in thy son, maiden, cold will his heart be ever, and there will be no warmth in his hands.' And Gallgoig—who knows not Gallgoig? 'Whatever township he came to, though there were three hundred homesteads therein, were he in need of aught, he would never leave sleep on man's eye whilst he was there.' When our author wants to dispatch no man is brisker than he. This is how he has Cilydd acquire a second wife. His first wife Goleuddydd has taken a promise of him that he will not marry again till he sees a two-headed briar growing on her grave, and a promise from her preceptor to strip the grave each year so that nothing can grow there. However, as preceptors will, he grows neglectful.

> One day when the king was hunting, he drew near the graveyard; he wanted to see the grave whereby he was to take a wife. He saw the briar. And when he saw it the king took counsel where he might get a wife. Quoth one of the counsellors, 'I could tell of a woman would suit thee well. She is the wife of king Doged.' They decided to seek her out. And they killed the king, and his wife they brought home with them, and an only daughter she had along with her; and they took possession of the king's lands (pp. 95–6).

This brusquerie, this hard nonchalance, often brutal, sometimes comic, is one of the hall-marks of our author, as witness the killing of Wrnach, the slicing of the Black Witch, Cyledyr's being forced to eat his father's heart, and the shaving and killing of Ysbaddaden:

And then Culhwch set forth, and Goreu son of Custennin with him, and everyone that wished ill to Ysbaddaden Chief Giant, and these marvels with him to his court. And Cadw of Prydein came to shave his beard, flesh, and skin to the bone, and his two ears outright. And Culhwch said, 'Hast had thy shave, man?' 'I have,' said he. 'And is thy daughter mine now?' 'Thine,' said he. . . . And then Goreu son of Custennin caught him by the hair of his head and dragged him behind him to the mound, and cut off his head, and set it on the bailey-stake (p. 136).

It would be idle to deny that our author is on occasion confused and confusing, staccato, truncated, giving us the impression that he is using some kind of shorthand or mnemonic. The proceedings at Custennin's mound and home lack clarity; Glewlwyd's bursts of oratory are wild, whirling, and windy. We shall have occasion later to notice that in the accomplishment of tasks he is both partial and arbitrary, and unsound on dogs into the bargain. It may be admitted that he stands naked to temptation to go one better than the best. Think of one fleet-footed man, Henwas the Winged (never a four-footed creature could run abreast of him the length of one acre, much less what would be farther than that), and he offers you three, Henwas (Old Servant), Henbeddestyr (Old Walker), and Sgilti Lightfoot, all of them brothers. If there is need for a hungry man, Huarwar (he was one of the three great plagues of Cornwall and Devon until his fill was found him), he cooks up three, Huarwar, Long Erwm and Long Atrwm (the day they came to a feast, three cantrefs would they seize for their needs; feasting till noon and drinking till night. When they went to sleep they would devour the heads of insects through hunger, as though they had never set tooth in food. When they went to a feast they left neither fat nor lean, neither hot nor cold, neither sour nor sweet, neither fresh nor salt, neither cooked nor raw). In this particular the heaviest censure directed against him has been in respect of the warriors at Arthur's court and the long-continuing list of tasks; but these, surely, require no defence, though later we may seek to provide one.

More immediately let us remark his skill in set-piece portraiture. His three main exercises in this area of his art relate to his hero Culhwch, his heroine Olwen, and his villain Ysbaddaden Chief Giant. There is a loving elaboration in the gallant picture of young Culhwch cantering to Arthur's court with his greyhounds sporting about him. The writing is loaded with rhetoric throughout:

Off went the boy on a steed with light-grey head, four winters old, with well-knit fork, shell-hoofed, and a gold tubular bridle-bit in its mouth. And under him a precious gold saddle, and in his hand two whetted spears of silver. A battle-axe in his hand, the fore-arm's length of a full grown man from ridge to edge. It would draw blood from the wind; it would be swifter than the swiftest dewdrop from the stalk to the ground, when the dew would be heaviest in the month of June. A gold-hilted sword on his thigh, and the blade of it gold, and a gold-chased buckler upon him, with the hue of heaven's lightning therein, and an ivory boss therein. And two greyhounds, white-breasted, brindled, in front of him, with a collar of red gold about the neck of either, from shoulder-swell to ear. The one that was on the left side would be on the right, and the one that was on the right side would be on the left, like two sea-swallows sporting around him. Four clods the four hoofs of his steed would cut, like four swallows in the air over his head, now before him, now behind him. A four-cornered mantle of purple upon him, and an apple of red gold in each of its corners; a hundred kine was the worth of each apple. The worth of three hundred kine in precious gold was there in his foot gear and his stirrups, from the top of his thigh to the tip of his toe. Never a hair-tip stirred upon him, so exceeding light his steed's canter under him on his way to the gate of Arthur's court[1] (p. 97).

It is interesting to see that our author does not devote so much as a word to Culhwch's person. Everything is externalized. That the boy is shapely and strong, handsome, gallant and brave, the youthful hero *par excellence*—this is conveyed by a telling sequence of association: horse, weapons, dogs, mantle, and foot-gear. Whether he is tall, short, thick, thin, raven-haired or pale as a leek, is at no

---

[1] Similar exercises in a highly wrought descriptive convention will be found elsewhere in the *Mabinogion* and extensively in Irish literature.

time indicated. Of his resplendent kind he is exactly as the reader's imagination would have him, son of a king of a rightful dominion, and worthy incumbent of Olwen's virgin bed.

The description of Olwen is no less formal, and even more stylized. We are told the colour of her hair and hands, her flesh and bosom, but she stays cool to view as a vellum manuscript or a wax doll. A clean doll, admittedly: 'She comes hither every Saturday to wash her head.' And an extravagant: 'And in the water where she washes she leaves all her rings.' And one most nobly similied:

She was sent for. And she came, with a robe of flame-red silk about her, and around the maiden's neck a torque of red gold, and precious pearls thereon and rubies. Yellower was her head than the flower of the broom, whiter was her flesh than the foam of the wave; whiter were her palms and her fingers than the shoots of the marsh trefoil from amidst the fine gravel of a welling spring. Neither the eye of the mewed hawk, nor the eye of the thrice-mewed falcon, not an eye was there fairer than hers. Whiter were her breasts than the breast of the white swan, redder were her cheeks than the reddest foxgloves. Whoso beheld her would be filled with love of her. Four white trefoils sprang up behind her wherever she went; and for that reason was she called Olwen[1] (pp. 110-1).

This is delicate, unparticularized, conventional, and professionally unemotive. If not wax, then a most charming piece of enamelling. Admirable of its kind, it invited the parody it received in *Peredur*, where it was the girl's teeth not her hair which were yellower than the flowers of the broom.

But it is our author's description of Ysbaddaden which is the most remarkable of the three set-pieces—if only because there is no description. By design or dereliction he is allowed to create himself. He is Ysbaddaden Penkawr, Chief or Head Giant, but we are not

---

[1] Olwen, White-track. As Culhwch (says our author) is Pig-run, because his mother ran off into the wilds, and came to her senses where a swineherd was keeping a herd of swine, and through terror of the swine the queen was delivered. The boy was named from the place where he was found. The authors of the *Mabinogion* are fond of such onomastic details and frequently invent them. *Olwen* probably means 'beautiful'.

instructed how big he is, or whether he is big at all. As with Grendel and Grendel's Mother, his size at any given moment is the size the story requires at that moment. His flock of sheep is without end or limit, his shepherd's mastiff is bigger than a nine-year-old stallion, and that same shepherd's wife can squeeze a wooden stake into a twisted withe. But the Giant's daughter, as folktale demands, is just a woman-sized woman waiting for a man-sized man to bed her in a bed-sized bed. And when he has been shaved so barbarously, Goreu catches him by the hair of his head and drags him off in what we assume to be a one-handed lugging sort of way before beheading him in the good old Celtic fashion. He is a determinedly sedentary giant—not that we are ever informed he is seated. He is just there, dominating his two sections of the story. This is a different and a higher art than our author devotes to Olwen. Where and how he lives, what he says and does, these things establish him. His dwelling is the greatest of forts in the world, into which Culhwch and the Companions make entry by killing nine gatemen who were at nine gates without a man crying out, and nine mastiffs without one squealing. They hold three savage, grotesque, but closely patterned interviews before the Giant states his terms. In each he fobs them with words, calls on those rascally servants and ruffians of his to raise up the forks under his drooping eyelids so that he may get sight of his future son-in-law.[1] In each he hurls a poisoned stone spear at them as they leave, in each they catch it and hurl it back, piercing him in three exquisitely painful places: the ball of his knee, the ball of his breast, and the ball of his eye—this last so deeply that it came out through the nape of the neck. In each he delivers himself of the invective appropriate to an injured Chief Giant. 'Thou cursed savage son-in-law! So long as I am left alive, the sight of my eyes will be the worse. When I go against the wind they will water,

---

[1] The shape, size, and nature of these eye-forks, in common with almost everything relating to Ysbaddaden, is never defined. When Miss Dorothea Braby was making her drawings for the Golden Cockerel *Mabinogion* (1948), like the translators she found Ysbaddaden's scale even more baffling than that of Brân the Blest, and contented herself with a portrayal of the head only. As for the forks (I quote): 'I have deliberately omitted the "eye-forks" as being altogether too obscure to convey'; and later, 'I decided he would have taken them out for his picture.'

a headache I shall have, and a giddiness each new moon. Cursed be the forge wherein it was heated! Like the bite of a mad dog to me the way the poisoned iron [*sic*] has pierced me.' In these scenes he is ranter and roarer, a fee-fi-fo-fumster who gives mouth like a belling bloodhound; but like the monster in human guise of a modern horror film he is made bearable by being made ridiculous, and is patently waiting on discomfiture and destruction.

Maybe the powerful impression we receive of Ysbaddaden Chief Giant is an unforeseen consequence of our author's inconsequentiality. More probably it reflects the Chief Giant's impressive role over many centuries of folktale. In any case the oblique method of his presentation is in direct contrast to the brilliantly particularized picture of Culhwch Eques and the flower-petal portrait of Olwen. That we are dealing with an accomplished and resourceful artist-remanieur is clear.

From such a man, whatever his virtues, and they are many, we shall not expect a flawless narrative. To use terms entirely meaningless to its artificer, *Culhwch and Olwen* shows no organic growth, has no inevitable architecture. One could take sentences out, or write sentences in, almost anywhere, and granted that one had a power of sentence-making equal to the original the result, though ill-advised, would fall short of desecration. If some parts of the narrative were transposed, only benefit would follow. A purist might object to various doublets, like the harangues attendant on entrance into both Arthur's and Wrnach's courts, the freeing of more than one prisoner, or the seeking of beard-removers from two boars, Ysgithyrwyn Chief Boar and Twrch Trwyth. For that there is a muddle over the tusk, razor, comb, and shears, their use and provenance, is abundantly evident. If the three sons of Cleddyf Difwlch won great fame at the slaying of Ysgithyrwyn we hear nothing of it at the time but are given the information by way of an entirely heedless afterthought; and other such disarticulations are not hard to find. In saying so much we are, of course, considering the story as we have it. If we knew more about its composition than we are ever likely to know, and were informed as to what extent the 'original' (whatever that means) has undergone change deliberate or inadvertent, orally or in writing, we might be able to acquit our author of some of the charges brought against him—or maybe arraign him with more.

Twice in *Culhwch and Olwen* he has attempted a wondrous-heroic (or for any to whom that word gives offence, a legendary) assemblage. The first is the muster of warriors at Arthur's court, the second the list of tasks, problems, marvels (*anoetheu*) set by Ysbaddaden. The court at which, and of which, Culhwch invokes his boon is a fantastic and exhilarating gathering. The old gods are there, euhemerized to men: Manawydan son of Llŷr, Gwyn son of Nudd, and Teyrnon Twryf Liant; there are the heroes earliest associated with Arthur— Cei and Bedwyr, Gereint and Gwalchmei (Gawain); the ladies Gwenhwyfar (Guenevere) and Gwenhwyach will be found, and the two Esyllts, she of the White Throat and she of the Slender. There are names which within inverted commas may be called 'historical', like Taliesin Chief of Bards and Cynwyl the Saint. Ireland sends her heroes, among them Cnychwr (Conchobar) son of Nes; Brittany a prince; and France three kings, including him after whom Paris was named. There are those in whom we surely discern the Strong Helpers of 'Six go through the World' now reduced as it were to qualities, or shall we say capacities, in human shape: Drem son of Dremidydd, Sight son of Seer, who saw from Cornwall to Pictland when a fly would rise in the morning with the sun; Clust son of Clustfeinad, Ear son of Hearer, who were he to be buried seven fathom in the earth would hear an ant fifty miles off when it stirred from its couch of a morning. Huarwar, we have seen, was a hungry man: he was one of the three great plagues of Cornwall and Devon until his fill was found him; no glimmer of a smile was ever to be seen on him save when he was sated. Sugyn was a thirsty: he would suck up the sea on which were three hundred ships till there remained only a dry strand; there was a red (i.e. scorching) breast-fever in him. There are the abstractions, Digon son of Alar (Enough son of Surfeit) and Nerth son of Cadarn (Might son of Strong); there is even Someone (Neb) with his eighteen brothers; and no less remarkable, the two whelps of the bitch Rhymhi. And Gwefyl son of Gwastad (on the day he was sad, one of his lips he would let down to his navel, and the other would be as a cowl on his head), Llwch Windy-hand, Osla Big-knife, Gilla Stag-shank, Henwas the

Winged, and the red-eye-stallion Llygadrudd Emys—a goblin lot
some of these, men of mark the others. And the plangent symphony
of the gold-torqued maidens: Celemon, Tangwen, Teleri, their
names are harp-notes and drip silver; fair Gwenlliant the magnanimous maiden, and Creiddylad, daughter of Lludd Silver-hand, the
maiden of most majesty that was ever in the Three Realms of Britain
and its three adjacent islands, and for her Gwythyr son of Greidawl
and Gwyn son of Nudd fight for ever each May calends till the day of
doom. In the name of all these did Culhwch invoke his boon, and
we need not be surprised that it was granted him.

The List of Tasks loses something of its extravagance if it is
studied as a Catalogue of Needs. A pattern, exuberant and heady
but fantastically apposite, may then be discerned. Meat and drink
and music are needed for Olwen's wedding feast; these are remarkable in their nature, and more remarkable for the means whereby
they can be secured. 'Dost see the great thicket yonder?' demands
Ysbaddaden.

I must have it uprooted out of the earth and burnt on the face of the
ground so that the cinders and ashes thereof be its manure; and that
it be ploughed and sown so that it be ripe in the morning against the
drying of the dew, in order that it may be made into meat and drink
for thy wedding guests and my daughter's. And all that I must have
done in one day.'

Out of this compulsion sprout five tasks. Only the Great Husband-
man can do the tilling; only the Great Artifex can set the irons; and
three legendary brace of oxen must be yoked to the plough. 'It is
easy for me to get that', replies Culhwch to each demand, 'though
thou think it is not easy'; and thirty-eight times Ysbaddaden
counters with a new article: 'Though thou get that, there is that
thou wilt not get'—and names it. No bride is complete without a
bridal head-dress.

'Dost see the hoed tilth yonder?' 'I see.' 'When first I met the
mother of that maiden, nine hestors of flax seed were sown therein;
neither black nor white has come out of it yet, and I have that measure
still. I must have that in the new-broken ground yonder, so that it

may be a white head-dress for my daughter's head on the day of thy wedding-feast.'

There must be honey that will be nine times sweeter than the honey of a virgin swarm, without drones and without bees, to make bragget for the feast; a cup to hold it, and a horn to pour it out. There must be a hamper of plenty, inexhaustible and all-providing, and music for the night: the harp of Teirtu, which will play of itself when a man so pleases, and when he so pleases be still; and the birds of Rhiannon, which wake the dead and lull the living to sleep. There must be the cauldron of Diwrnach the Irishman, to boil meat for the wedding guests. So many needs, so many owners, most of them hostile or unwilling, and of the remainder most lost, unknown, unseizable. Even before we reach the impossible demands which spring from the hunting of Twrch Trwyth, Ysbaddaden's shave presents problems. He must be shaved with a tusk from the head of Ysgithyrwyn Chief Boar. It must be plucked from his head while alive. No one in the world can so pluck it save the hero named for the purpose; and only a second named hero can be entrusted with its safe-keeping. And, 'Though thou get that, there is that thou wilt not get. I must needs dress my beard for me to be shaved. It will never settle unless the blood of the Black Witch be obtained, daughter of the White Witch, from the head of the Valley of Grief in the uplands of Hell.' By the beard of my friend (as the *Mabinogion* would say), most formidable; but the tasks of wondertales are set only that they may be accomplished, and to every one of them Culhwch makes response in the same brisk and confident manner.

That the list of warriors could be tidier, and the list of requirements more orderly, may be granted. Beyond that, critical severity is out of place. For these two are enough in themselves to make *Culhwch and Olwen* a granary bursting with the golden grain of Celtic tradition. One reads them with the sensation that here, tantalizingly glimpsed, is a heaped-up treasure-house of half-known or unknown Welsh story. It would be rash to read into every nickname, each ascription, and every reference to matters untraced, the hint of a saga or even an anecdote lost; but we know from the triads, the Stanzas of the Graves, from brevities in Nennius and amplifications in Geoffrey of Monmouth, from references to bards and story-tellers, and from the lore demanded of the analogous Irish *ollamh*, that a big corpus of story, in large degree of ancient lineage, was known to medieval Wales, though comparatively little of it has survived. In the list of warriors we can postulate errors, and what in the genetical sciences are called sports, but this is no great matter: we can safely give a little to win a lot. When our author brings in (even drags in) Gwyn son of Nudd and the daughter of Lludd Silver-hand, or Nyniaw and Peibiaw, whom God transformed into oxen for their sins, he little delays and greatly enriches his action, quickens it, multiplies its areas of reference and levels of meaning. It is our further good fortune that the two assemblages and their dependent matter provide the opportunity for so many of those pregnant expressions, clinching sentences, and thumbnail sketches which are a main feature of his art. To these *Culhwch and Olwen* owes much of its salt and savour; and if they are faults (which to me they are not) they are the faults of life and abundance, not of dearth and mortuary prudence.

To conclude this part of the argument, *Culhwch and Olwen*, when we see it whole, and seek no impossible architectonics, is a surprisingly well-ordered narrative. It begins at the beginning and ends at the end, and in between, if its details are sometimes staccato and its effects disjointed, it moves both itself and its readers. Culhwch's birth, the provision of a stepmother, the destiny sworn on him, the recourse to Arthur, the listing of Arthur's warriors, the promise of help, the first unsuccessful search for Olwen, the enlistment of the helping companions, the finding of Olwen, the interviews with Ysbaddaden Chief Giant, the naming of the tasks, the achievement of some of them, the death of the giant, and the marriage of Culhwch and his white-palmed bride—true, this is no majestic, smooth-flowing river of narrative, cabined and confined, but it is an exciting, at times hair-raising succession of freshets, cataracts, and rapids, transporting us through a variegated, spectacular, part-real, and part-magical landscape.

2. Achieving the Tasks

So FAR WE HAVE DEFERRED EXAMINATION OF THAT substantial portion of *Culhwch and Olwen* (it comes to more than a third) which treats of the accomplishment of the tasks imposed on Culhwch and his helpers by Ysbaddaden Chief Giant. This is not through any lack of engagement with the material. On the contrary, the pages that tell of Mabon and the Oldest Animals, and of the hunting of the boar Twrch Trwyth, are among the most compelling in the *Mabinogion*.

We have already remarked that the accomplishment of the tasks is discharged in a partial and arbitrary manner. Some two-thirds of them go by default, in that they are covered by a general statement of Arthur's and one of his men. It is possible that our author deliberately left a framework for other story-tellers to fill in; maybe what we now possess is a mutilated and shortened version of his grand design, or even an interpolated one; but it is altogether more likely that the *anoetheu*, the marvels and tasks, were simply not tackled by him in their entirety. Such an encyclopedia of Welsh, Celtic, Indo-European, international, universal folktale and legend was surely beyond his powers or his intention.

We have likewise remarked the 'hard nonchalance, often brutal, sometimes comic', characteristic of our author. This is nowhere more apparent than in the accomplishment of tasks. Beowulf, we noticed (p. 49), acts as the agent of religion, justice, and moral right when he discharges his folklore tasks so ruthlessly on the bodies of the god-forsaken monsters who raid Heorot. He is a good man disposing of evil, and has our sympathy undivided. In *Culhwch and Olwen* one can hardly speak of sympathy. The tasks are achieved not

because they are just, desirable in themselves, or beneficial to mankind. They are achieved because the story requires that they be
achieved, and right and wrong are swallowed up in necessity.
Before he begins to help Arthur, Gwyn ap Nudd has made his foe
and prisoner, Cyledyr son of Nwython, eat his father's heart. Cei
and Bedwyr, Goreu and Arthur are no less void of mercy's milk or
pity's qualm. The Helping Companions use their gifts, display their
qualities, fulfil their functions, and that these involve ferocity,
cunning, treachery, the abuse of hospitality and the most revolting
cruelty, troubles the narrator not one whit. His relish of the action
is unflagging throughout, and when the story demands it he kills
off his own side with the same zest as he splits, skewers, carves,
plucks, or flays the enemy. Neither means nor end are ever questioned. His work is as far from compassion as from moral purpose, and
it is a tribute to his powers of literary execution that the final effect
of his masterpiece is not to lay a hand colder than Cei's on the
reader's breast.

The pleasant little folktale of the helpful ants, itself a version of
the Grateful Animals, starts a shade awkwardly, proceeds with precision, and ends like a charm.[1] The plucking out of Dillus's beard
by the cold Cei and fearsome Bedwyr (its hairs are needed to make
a leash, and must be plucked out while he is still alive, and with
wooden tweezers too, for dead they would be brittle) is handled with
the high-spirited heartlessness dear to our author. A murderous
raid into Ireland secures the cauldron of Diwrnach. There is a gruesome but comic irreverence in the obtaining of the blood of the
Black Witch; the slaughter of Wrnach the Giant and the killing of

---

[1] 'And as Gwythyr son of Greidawl was one day journeying over a mountain,
he heard a wailing and a grievous lamentation, and these were a horrid noise
to hear. He sprang forward in that direction, and when he came there he
drew his sword and smote off the anthill level with the ground, and so saved
them from the fire. And they said to him, "Take thou God's blessing and ours,
and that which no man can ever recover, we will come and recover it for thee."
It was they thereafter who came with the nine hestors of flax seed which
Ysbaddaden Chief Giant had named to Culhwch, in full measure, with none
of it wanting save for a single flax seed. And the lame ant brought that in
before night' (*Mabinogion* p. 127). The theme itself is widely dispersed
throughout Europe and Asia as part of the Magic Flight and the Grateful
Animals, but the lame ant is thought to be a Welsh benediction.

Ysgithyrwyn the boar are unscrupulous and savage respectively, cunning and brisk; to the Unending Battle we shall refer in the context of the British Arthur; but it is on the two tasks which involve the Freeing of the Prisoner and the Hunting of the Otherworld Boar that our author has put forth the full measure of his strength.

Of Mabon son of Modron we are told that he was taken away when three nights old from betwixt his mother and the wall, since when nothing has been heard of him, not even whether he is alive or dead, much less his whereabouts. But now he must be obtained by Arthur and his men, for 'there is no huntsman in the world can act as houndsman to the hound Drudwyn, save he.' But Ysbaddaden is an ogre for complications, and Mabon will never be found unless his kinsman Eidoel is found. Unfortunately Eidoel is in Glini's prison, so Glini too has to be found, and won over. By now the quest for Olwen has lasted two years. Glini found, Eidoel found, Mabon stays lost as ever. Counsel is taken of the birds and beasts, and more specifically of the Oldest Animals. First Arthur's messengers come to the Blackbird of Cilgwri, so aged that with his beak he has whittled away a smith's anvil, till only a small nut of iron remains. He knows nothing of Mabon, but leads the messengers on to the Stag of Rhedynfre. The Stag has seen a sapling grow into an oak tree with a hundred branches, then fall and diminish to a red and rusty stock; but he knows nothing of Mabon, and takes them on to the still older Owl of Cwm Cawlwyd, who has outlived three successive forests and whose wings have become withered stumps. But he has never heard of Mabon. So in his turn he guides them to the oldest and widest-travelled creature in the world, the Eagle of Gwernabwy. The Eagle has sat on a rock and pecked at the stars each evening till the rock is not a handbreadth in height, but he knows nothing of Mabon. But once upon a time he went to seek his meat as far as Llyn Llyw, and there struck his claws into a Salmon, thinking he would be meat for him many a long day, but the Salmon dragged him down into the depths, and it was with difficulty that he got away. Perhaps the Salmon of Llyn Llyw would know?[1] And

---

[1] Early listeners to the story would feel assured of it. The Salmon was a traditional repository of knowledge. What the dragon Fafnir was to Sigurd,

from that venerable fish, his back scarred with fifty tridents, they
learn of a prisoner who lamented his incarceration at Caer Loyw,
Gloucester on the Severn, and Cei and Gwrhyr Interpreter of
Tongues (that cunning, cold, ferocious Cei whom later tradition
would degrade to a rudester and buffoon) travelled on the Salmon's
shoulders and talked with him through the wall.

And Cei and Gwrhyr Interpreter of Tongues went upon the salmon's
shoulders, and they journeyed until they came to the far side of the
wall from the prisoner, and they could hear wailing and lamentation
on the far side of the wall from them. Gwrhyr said, 'What man
laments in this house of stone?' 'Alas, man, there is cause for him who
is here to lament. Mabon son of Modron is here in prison; and none
was ever so cruelly imprisoned in a prison house as I; neither the
imprisonment of Lludd Silver-hand nor the imprisonment of Greid
son of Eri.' 'Hast thou hope of getting thy release for gold or for
silver or for worldly wealth, or by battle and fighting?' 'What is got
of me, will be got by fighting.'
   They returned thence and came to where Arthur was. They told
where Mabon son of Modron was in prison. Arthur summoned the
warriors of this Island and went to Caer Loyw where Mabon was in
prison. Cei and Bedwyr went upon the shoulders of the fish. Whilst
Arthur's warriors assaulted the fort, Cei broke through the wall and
took the prisoner on his back; and still he fought with the men.
Arthur came home and Mabon with him, a free man (*Mabinogion*,
p. 126).

Who was this Mabon? Even as one of the Three Exalted Prisoners
of the Island of Britain he is no ordinary man, and once upon a time
he was a god. Altars are to be found in Great Britain and on the

---

the salmon of Féc's Pool was to Finn. When Sigurd had killed the dragon and
was roasting its heart he touched it with his finger and put the finger to
his mouth to ease its smart. At once he understood the language of birds.
When Finn was cooking Féc's salmon, under strict orders not to eat it, he
likewise burned his thumb and set it to his mouth, and by that means acquired
wisdom. Sigurd-Siegfried's affinities with Finn and other Celtic heroes are
many and strong. For a brief discussion of his position in Celto-Germanic
tradition see E. O. G. Turville-Petre, *Myth and Religion of the North*, 1964, pp.
203–4; for an account and interpretation of Finn see T. F. O'Rahilly, *Early
Irish History and Mythology*, Dublin, 1946, pp. 318 ff.

Continent of Europe raised to Mabon, or Maponos as he was then called, and to Modron, Matrona, his mother, with their names inscribed upon them. From these we know that by the Romans Maponos was identified with Apollo. So Mabon son of Modron, Maponos son of Matrona, is, or was, the Son of the Mother: Son-God, Boy-God, and Mother-Goddess, distant deities of the migratory Celts, still remembered though much transmuted in Gaul and Britain. It has been argued, therefore, that with Mabon and his taking away when three nights old from betwixt his mother and the wall, we deal with a myth like the Sumerian tradition relating to Tammuz and Inanna, or Persephóne daughter of Demeter, whose abduction in the fields of Enna by gloomy Dis robbed earth of its increase and joy. If so, by the time of the Welsh manuscripts the myth of Mabon has undergone great changes; it has been localized, and rationalized, so that Mabon's Otherworld prison or home becomes a house of stone at Gloucester; the story has been drawn into the earliest Arthurian assemblage; and by accident or design, in either case operating with the effect of genius, the story of Mabon has been blended with the folktale of the Oldest Animals, and later with that of the Great Hunt. In brief, the myth has ceased to have significance, and as myth may have ceased to exist. What is moving in this part of *Culhwch and Olwen* derives rather from the Oldest Animals, whose grave benevolence, stateliness, repose, and self-sufficiency strike the heart with such sensations as affect us before the standing stones, the burial chambers, the hill forts, and religious places of our ancestors.[1]

---

[1] As man increasingly denies himself communion and contact with animals and birds, save for a limited sentimentality on the one hand and an unlimited exploitation on the other, inevitably he finds it ever harder to comprehend their insistent role in the lives and beliefs of his forebears. In early Celtic and Germanic religion there appears to have been a connection, though hard to isolate and define, between gods and beasts, the bull, bear, stag, horse, boar among them. In the accompanying mythologies there were animals attached to, or sacred to, the gods. Legends and folktale abound in stories of shape-shifting and transformation, from India to Ireland, from the North Cape to the Pillars of Hercules. And of course far wider. Many a hero of the Celtic world is born simultaneously with an animal: Pryderi with a colt, Cúchulainn with two, Finn with a dog, Lug with twelve half-brothers who become seals, and Lleu with Dylan eil Ton, Sea son of Wave, who makes instantly for his

II. MOMENT OF TRUTH: DOG MEETS BEAST
From Caerleon

One might at this point of the story wonder how even the most gifted writer could avoid some sinking or slackening in what is to come. No man can give better than his best. But one learns of this particular author that he has many kinds of best, and like the cunning, fortunate artist he was he has kept his *tour de force* to the last. The hunting of Twrch Trwyth, Porcus Troit, seems to have been known to the author of the *Gorchan* or Lay of Cynfelyn associated with the *Gododdin*, and was touched by Nennius in the eighth or ninth century in his list of the *mirabilia* of Britain in his *Historia Brittonum*. So early the feat is ascribed to Arturus Miles, Arthur the Warrior, but the marvel is a heap of stones on which lies a stone bearing the imprint of the foot of Arthur's dog Cafall.[1] In *Culhwch and Olwen* the marvel for today's reader is the Hunting of the Boar.

---

native element, receives its nature, then swims there as well as the best fish in the sea. Heroes are suckled by beasts, or named after an animal connection: Culhwch because he was born in a pig-run, Cúchulainn 'the hound of Culann', and Mes Buachalla, 'Cowherds' Fosterchild'. Many were born of swan maidens, and such feathered brides are plentiful in the world's folktales. As we shall see in the story of Diarmaid a hero's life might be coterminous with that of a fated beast, in that they are doomed to kill each other (pp. 104–5). Saints, equally with heroes, were happy to acknowledge an animal kinship. 'St Ailbe, suckled by a wolf, acknowledged to the end of his days this "kinship by the milk"; St Ciwa, suckled in the same way, had a great nail like a wolf's claw on one of her fingers and was called the "Wolf Girl"' (Alwyn Rees and Brinley Rees, *Celtic Heritage, Ancient Tradition in Ireland and Wales*, 1961, p. 232, a work on which I have drawn heavily for this note). That animals and birds should think and talk and be causative in the life and thought of men was acceptable on both the natural and supernatural plane. We may note too the frequency with which men of mould, as well as heroes, were named from the animal world: Wolf, Bear, Boar, Horse, Deer, Hound, Serpent, Bull and Eagle, and their rich and numerous derivatives in the Celtic and Germanic tongues.

1 'There is another marvel in the region which is called Buelt (Buellt, Builth). There is there a heap of stones, and one stone placed on top of the heap with the footprint of a dog in it. When he was hunting Porcus Troit (Troynt), Cabal (Cafall), who was the dog of Arthur the Warrior, impressed the stone with his footprint, and Arthur later collected a heap of stones under this stone in which was the footprint of his dog, and it is called Carn Cabal (Carn Cafallt). And men come and carry away the stone in their hands for the space of a day and a night, and on the next day it will be found back on its heap.'
Cafall (Cabal) is probably the name of a horse, as *carn* is a hoof rather than a paw.

12. THE GUNDESTRUP CAULDRON
Panel showing a god with beasts and a man riding on a fish.

Let us begin with a renewed consideration of the catalogue of tasks, where Twrch Trwyth is responsible for no fewer than nineteen of the two-score entries. The catalogue, we have said, is a much more precise document than is commonly assumed, concerned first with the wedding feast, entertainment, and bridal head-dress, second with the shaving of Ysbaddaden, and third with the dressing of his hair. His hair may be dressed only with the comb and shears from between the ears of Twrch Trwyth the wondrous boar. 'He will not give them of his own free will, nor canst thou compel him.' But the boar cannot be hunted without the whelp Drudwyn; there is no leash in the world to hold Drudwyn save the leash of Cors Hundred-claws; the only collar for that leash is the collar of Canhastyr Hundred-hands; the only chain for that collar is the chain of Cilydd Hundred-holds. Fortunately for all concerned, these three worthies belong or have been made to belong to Arthur's court. There is no huntsman who can hunt with Drudwyn save Mabon son of Modron. Mabon cannot be found unless his kinsman Eidoel is found first; no horse save Gwyn Dun-mane can carry Mabon. That makes eight tasks so far, and before we finish we arrive at six stipulations as to dogs and their harness; two as to horses; just one as to weapons; and no fewer than nine as to huntsmen or groups of huntsmen—including Arthur and the warriors of his court. For if we ponder what I may call the Great Hunt in literature we shall find that in this part of his story our author had little more freedom of manoeuvre than the hound Drudwyn on his leash, collar, and chain.

When the exploit gets under way Twrch Trwyth lay in Ireland. Arthur's first overture is rebuffed with pig-eyed rancour and a shower of poison. And then Arthur gathered together what warriors there were in the Three Realms of Britain and its three adjacent islands, and what there were in France and Brittany and Normandy and the Summer Country, and what there were of picked dogs and horses of renown. And with all those hosts he went to Ireland. And with those men and those dogs he engaged with the Boar and his seven piglings. As we speculate who and what Twrch Trwyth was, Arthur gives us this answer. 'He was a king, and for his wickedness God transformed him into a swine.' He was a royal beast, then, as

well as an uncanny—and in the old and frightening biblical sense,
a hardened sinner. A tumbled monarch out of love with words, so
that it is his son Grugyn Silver-bristle[1] who makes answer to
Arthur's bidding that he, Twrch Trwyth, should in God's name
come and talk to him. 'Harm enough hath God wrought us, to have
made us in this shape, without you too coming to fight with us. . . .
And tomorrow in the morning we will set out hence and go to
Arthur's country, and there we will do all the mischief we can.'
Ireland ravaged in three pitched battles, and but one pigling slain,
Twrch Trwyth and his brood swam the sea to ravage Wales.[2]
Arthur and his host, his horses and his dogs, went aboard the ship
Prydwen and followed them to Porth Cleis in Pembrokeshire, and
then overland through South Wales to the Wye and Severn, by a
route so closely delineated that the curious may follow their tracks
to this day. Time after time they were brought to bay, and always
they slew and broke through. Then pig by pig they fell, with a toll
of heroes around them, till at last only Twrch Trwyth and his sons
Grugyn Silver-bristle and Llwydawg the Hewer were left alive. No
barrow-pigs, *porci castrati* these, but a match for the bravest and
strongest of the Island of Britain. A king of France and a king of
Brittany, Arthur's two uncles and his one son, three of his porter's
porters, and his head builder, they were slashed and dashed, tusked
and kneaded. Crashing through brakes, wheeling in the forests,
shaggy with spears and festooned with dogs, the three survivors

[1] 'Like wings of silver were all his bristles; what way he went through wood
and meadow one could discern from how his bristles glittered.' Farther north
the god Frey had a boar named Golden-bristle (Gullinbursti), who could run
faster than a horse over air or sea and whose bristles shed radiance on the
darkest night.
[2] Twrch Trwyth and his progeny were tremendous swimmers, in sea and
river. Though hardly more so than Henwen, Old-white, the sow of Dadweir
Blind-head, who made her way from the headland of Austin in Cornwall to
the Menai Straits (see p. 109n.). The notion that pigs cut their throats with
their hooves when swimming can never have derived from the lean boar of
the wild. In my last footnote I mentioned Gullinbursti, and would here
mention the huge old boar Beigad, Fear-bringer or Terrifier, who serviced
Ingimund the Old's lost herd in Svinadal in the north of Iceland. When they
tried to catch him he took to the water and swam till his hooves dropped off,
but even so got himself to land, to a hill, before relinquishing his porcine ghost
(*Vatnsdœla Saga*, c. 15; *Landnámabók*, c. 226).

maintain the battle. 'Their snouts dig sepulchres where'er they go.' Their terms are life for life, there is no begging-off for hunters or hunted. Then Silver-bristle was brought down in a ring of slain, and Garth Grugyn for ever marks the place of his quell; and the Hewer, heaped with royal and avuncular spoil, fell at Ystrad Yw.

Twrch Trwyth went then between Tawy and Ewyas. Arthur summoned Cornwall and Devon to meet him at the mouth of the Severn. And Arthur said to the warriors of this Island: 'Twrch Trwyth has slain many of my men. By the valour of men, not while I am alive shall he go into Cornwall. I will pursue him no further, but I will join with him life for life. You, do what you will.' And by his counsel a body of horsemen was sent, and the dogs of the Island with them, as far as Ewyas, and they beat back thence to the Severn, and they waylaid him there with what tried warriors there were in this Island, and drove him by sheer force into Severn. And Mabon son of Modron went with him into Severn, on Gwyn Dun-mane the steed of Gweddw, and Goreu son of Custennin and Menw son of Teirgwaedd, between Llyn Lliwan and Aber Gwy. And Arthur fell upon him, and the champions of Britain along with him. Osla Big-knife drew near, and Manawydan son of Llŷr, and Cacamwri, Arthur's servant, and Gwyngelli, and closed in on him. And first they laid hold of his feet, and soused him in Severn till it was flooding over him. On the one side Mabon son of Modron spurred his horse and took the razor from him [for there is a razor between his ears now too], and on the other Cyledyr the Wild, on another horse, plunged into Severn with him and took from him the shears. But or ever the comb could be taken he found land with his feet; and from the moment he found land neither dog nor man nor horse could keep up with him until he went into Cornwall. Whatever mischief was come by in seeking those treasures from him, worse was come by in seeking to save the two men from drowning. Cacamwri, as he was dragged forth, two quern-stones dragged him into the depths. As Osla Big-knife was running after the boar, his knife fell out of its sheath. And he lost it; and his sheath thereafter being full of water, as he was dragged forth, it dragged him back into the depths.

Then Arthur went with his hosts until he caught up with him in Cornwall. Whatever mischief was come by before that was play to what was come by then in seeking the comb. But from mischief to mischief the comb was won from him. And then he was forced out of

Cornwall and driven straight forward into the sea. From that time forth never a one has known where he went, and Aned and Aethlem with him. And Arthur went thence to Celli Wig in Cornwall, to bathe himself and rid him of his weariness (pp. 37-8).

This is fine narrative, gallant, comic, beautiful, deadly, zestful, hard, heady, and precise. The hunting of a mighty beast has been a recurrent and compelling theme in the literature and pictorial art of that most dedicated and destructive of all hunters, Man. Men of talent have given it their best, and men of genius their all. It is a tribute to the art of *Culhwch and Olwen* that with the hunting of Twrch Trwyth it offers us one of the most memorable examples of the genre.

3. Arthur with Warriors

To say something accurate, significant, yet brief about the British Arthur is among the most testing of the *anoetheu*, the wondrous tasks, laid upon the expositor of *Culhwch and Olwen*.

We can begin by setting aside the historical (if we agree that there was an historical[1]) Arthur. The Arthur of *Culhwch and Olwen* is not an historical personage, and nothing he does there is related to history. He is neither king (*brenin*) of a kingdom, nor emperor (*ameraudur*) of an empire. For the most part his men call him Arthur, rarely lord (*arglwydd*), and Culhwch's resonant greeting, 'Hail, sovereign prince (*or* sovereign ruler) of this Island (*penteyrned yr ynys hon*)', is neither repeated by its deliverer nor emulated by its hearers. Nor is he the gracious, glorious monarch of later tradition who has taken more than Christendom for his fief and shaken out his shoe from Taprobane to Greenland. He is not even the Arthur of the three Arthurian romances of the *Mabinogion*, with their deep grain of Norman-French influence. Rather he is the British Arthur, revealed to us not in French, German, or English material, but in

---

[1] It is probable that there was, but the evidence is scanty and arguable. It may be read in E. K. Chambers, *Arthur of Britain*, 1927, and in translation in R. L. Brengle (ed.), *Arthur King of Britain*, New York, 1964. There are brief but important statements in R. G. Collingwood and J. N. L. Myres, *Roman Britain and the English Settlements*, 1937; R. S. Loomis (ed.), *Arthurian Literature in the Middle Ages*, 1959 (the relevant sections are Kenneth H. Jackson, 'The Arthur of History' and 'Arthur in Early Welsh Verse'); John J. Parry, 'The Historical Arthur', in JEGPh. LVIII, 1959; and Thomas Jones, 'Datblygiadau Cynnar Chwedl Arthur', in BBCS, 1958, trans. Gerald Morgan, 'The Early Evolution of the Legend of Arthur', Nottingham Mediaeval Studies VIII, 1964.

British (which in this connection means Welsh) material uncontaminated by the Cycles of Romance, though necessarily affected by the vast and, in respect of Wales, partly forgotten complex of Celtic myth, wondertale, and legend.

Fortunately we possess sources of information about this British Arthur, apart from *Culhwch and Olwen*, though they are more than normally difficult to interpret and assess. First we may note that Arthur and many who were to be associated with him in the development of his legend were early reported on by the poets of *Englynion y Beddau*, 'The Stanzas of the Graves', also known as *Beddau Milwyr Ynys Prydein*, 'The Graves of the Warriors of the Island of Britain', the longest sequence of which is preserved in the early thirteenth-century Black Book of Carmarthen, though the englynion themselves are believed to be products of the ninth century or the tenth. Among those whose graves receive mention there are Arthur, Bedwyr, Gwalchmei, Cynon, Gwythur son of Greidawl, Gwgawn Red-sword, March (presumably king Mark), but not Cei. The grave of Gwalchmei, we read, is in Peryddon, 'as a reproach to men'; the grave of Bedwyr is on Tryfan hill (the stanza mentions Camlan, the battle which proved fatal to Arthur and Medraut-Modred in, says the the tenth-century *Annales Cambriae*, the year 537–9). The most famous stanza of all refers to three of Arthur's entourage and to Arthur himself:

> Bet y March, bet y Guythur,
> bet y Gugaun Cledyfrut;
> anoeth bid bet y Arthur.

Which may be rendered:

> A grave for March, a grave for Gwythur,
> A grave for Gwgawn Red-sword;
> The world's wonder a grave for Arthur.[1]

In other words, Arthur's grave is a universal mystery, its whereabouts unknown to men, and unknown, one is tempted to think,

[1] For a text, translation, and discussion of this poetic material see Thomas Jones, 'The Black Book of Carmarthen "Stanzas of the Graves"', Sir John Rhys Memorial Lecture, British Academy, 1967.

because of the belief that Arthur was not dead and would in time return to his people. A line in the *Gododdin*, if we could be sure that it is not a later interpolation, suggests that Arthur was very early (*c*. 600, 900?) a fixed point for heroic comparison, for of one of the doomed men who rode to Catraeth we hear that 'though he was not Arthur' he glutted black ravens on the fortress-wall; and a stanza of an early poem about Gereint ab Erbin preserved in the Black Book of Carmarthen refers to Arthur 'the emperor, strife's commander' hewing with steel at the battle of Llongborth, Langport on the river Parret in Somerset. In the so-called *Preideu Annwfyn*, 'The Spoils of Annwn', from the thirteenth-century Book of Taliesin, we hear of Arthur's raids in his ship Prydwen on eight caers in the Otherworld.

> Perfect was the imprisonment of Gweir in Caer Siddi,
> According to the Tale of Pwyll and Pryderi;
> No one before him went to it . . .
> Three freights of Prydwen went we into it,
> Save seven none came back from Caer Siddi.

In the second verse there is mention of the Cauldron of the Head of Annwn, which 'boils not the food of a coward'.

> And when we went with Arthur, famed disaster,
> Save seven none came back from Caer Feddwyd.

In the fifth we hear of the Ych Brych, the 'Speckled Ox' of *Culhwch and Olwen*.

> And when we went with Arthur, grievous visit,
> Save seven none came back from Caer Fandwy.

And so to the last verse:

> When we went with Arthur, grievous contest,
> Save seven none came back from Caer Ochren

In this context belongs the poem beginning *Golychafi gulwyd*, and that beginning *Pa gur*, 'What man?', contained in the early thirteenth-century Black Book of Carmarthen (pp. 94–6)—though the poem is considerably older than the manuscript itself. In *Pa gur* we find Arthur seeking entry into a 'house' of which Glewlwyd Mighty-grasp is porter.

> A. What man is porter?
> G. Glewlwyd Mighty-grasp.
>   What man asks it?
> A. Arthur and Cei Wyn.
> G. Who goes along with thee?
> A. The best men in the world.
> G. Into my house thou shalt not come
>   Unless thou disclose them.
> A. I will disclose them,
>   And thou shalt see them.

And so Arthur names his followers: Mabon son of Modron, Cysteint son of Banon, Gwyn Godyfrion, Manawydan son of Llŷr ('of profound counsel'), Mabon son of Mellt, Anwas the Winged, Llwch Windy-hand, Bedwyr Four-teeth and Llacheu. As in *Culhwch and Olwen* pride of place is given to Cei and his exploits. Here too he is the famed warlock-warrior.

> Cei pleaded with them
> While he slew them three by three . . .
> Though Arthur was but playing,
> Blood was flowing
> In the hall of Wrnach (Afarnach?)
> Fighting with a hag . . .
> An army was vanity
> Compared with Cei in battle . . .
> When he drank from a horn
> He would drink as much as four;
> Into battle when he came
> He slew as would a hundred.
> Unless God should accomplish it,
> Cei's death would be unattainable.
> Cei Wyn and Llacheu
> They used to make battles

Before the pangs of the blue spears . . .
Cei pierced nine witches.
Cei Wyn went to Môn
To kill lions.
Polished was his shield
Against Palug's Cat . . .
Nine score warriors
Would fall as food for her. . . .

Clearly these poems and *Culhwch and Olwen* are much of a piece. They tell of the same people, and when not that, of people of the same kind, and the events described are of a kind: freeing a prisoner, raiding a stronghold, carrying off a cauldron, and hunting wild beasts. Nothing in the Glewlwyd dialogue would be out of place in the prose narrative: the bloodied hall of Wrnach, the slaughter of hags, monsters, witches. Cei, Bedwyr, and Gwalchmei are consistent figures throughout, and hardly to be recognized in the persons bearing those names in later romance. Sir Kay the Seneschal is a boor and a buffoon, very much the discourteous fool. It is his role to give a rude welcome, muddle a quest, attack beyond his strength, and be knocked flat for his pains. He acts like some pallid and enfeebled understudy of Bricriu, Cúroi, or the northern Loki. But the earlier Cei is a towering, formidable figure, unconquerable by man or beast.[1] He is the first of Arthur's train, a warlock and shapeshifter; he can live under water or go without sleep nine nights and nine days; the wound he deals is mortal; he can be tall as a tree or render things invisible. We have earlier marked him as a cold and cunning creature (see pp. 72 and 83 above). It is Cei who leads Culhwch to Ysbaddaden's court, Cei who slays Wrnach the Giant, it is on Cei's back that Mabon is carried to his freedom, and it was Cei who planned and with Bedwyr executed the plucking of Dillus's beard. A queer thing followed:

And then the two of them went to Celli Wig in Cornwall, and a leash from Dillus the Bearded's beard with them. And Cei gave it into Arthur's hand, and thereupon Arthur sang this englyn:

[1] Though among the warriors or names invoked by Culhwch at Arthur's court we hear of Gwyddawg son of Menestyr, who slew Cei (and Arthur then slew him and his brothers to avenge Cei).

Cei made a leash
From Dillus's beard, son of Euri.
Were he alive, thy death he'd be.

And because of this Cei grew angry, so that it was with difficulty the warriors of this Island made peace between Cei and Arthur. But nevertheless, neither for Arthur's lack of help nor for the slaying of his men, did Cei have aught to do with him in his hour of need from that time forward (p. 128).

For the rest of *Culhwch and Olwen* this is simple truth. He disappears from the tale, though the slicing of the Black Witch, so that she was as two tubs, would seem just the job for him. 'Wher artow Gawyn the curtesse and Cay the crabed?' Was it not some such tradition of his cantankerousness in Welsh story which led to the unhappy metamorphosis of the romances?

Gawain's destiny was the opposite of Cei's. In *Culhwch and Olwen* Gwalchmei-Gawain receives no commendations for courtesy. Arthur called on him 'because he never came home without the quest he had gone to seek. He was the best of walkers and the best of riders. He was Arthur's nephew, his sister's son, and his first cousin.' Very much a Strong Helper of folktale. But in the later romances of the *Mabinogion* he shows a high polish. The best-known passage in *Peredur* tells how the hero saw a she-hawk kill a duck on snow which had fallen overnight; then a raven alighted on the bird's flesh, and Peredur, observing it, fell into a meditation. 'I was thinking of the lady I love best', he explained to Gwalchmei. 'This is the reason why remembrance thereof came to me. I was looking on the snow and the raven, and the blood-drops of the duck which the she-hawk had killed in the snow. And I was thinking how similar was the exceeding whiteness of her flesh to the snow, and the exceeding blackness of her hair and her brows to the raven, and the two red spots that were in her cheeks to the two drops of blood.' Gwalchmei, 'with his olde curteisye', hears him out with patience and approval: 'Those were not ungentle thoughts', and thinks it not excessive that he should break Cei's arm and shoulder-blade and trample him under his horse's hooves twenty-one times for interrupting such knightly rumination.

The world of *Culhwch and Olwen* is folktale, wondrous and cruel. The place-names and compass-bearings refer to South Wales, Cornwall, and Ireland, but the spiritual geography is often that of Annwn, the Celtic Otherworld, while its inhabitants seem sometimes more and sometimes less than human. Arthur's name in the *Historia Brittonum* is a gleam in a dark place, but this is not the Arthur of *Culhwch and Olwen*, that fabulous barbaric chieftain of a barbarous fantastic court, whose rule and realm are of the mind. In *Culhwch* his position in British story is already secure, and hero after hero has been drawn into his train. Time has already made him the magnet to whom wondertales and legendary exploits have been attracted. He is the beneficent folk hero. This is a process of accretion too well known to need documentation: in the Matter of Britain it will grow ever easier for adventures to touch on Arthur, through his men. The pattern has begun to reveal itself, the pattern that would dominate Arthurian romance, of adventures that start at Arthur's court but are carried out by Gawain, Galahad, Lancelot, Perceval, whom you will, as in the older *Culhwch and Olwen* they are in large measure carried out by such indubitably Welsh heroes as Cei and Bedwyr, Gwalchmei, Menw the spell-caster, and Gwrhyr Interpreter of Tongues. Just how and when some of these squeezed their way into the internationally dispersed folktale, 'Six go through the World' is not clear. But that they did so is in no way surprising. In order that the hero shall obtain the giant's or king's daughter, who wishes to be so obtained, and gives counsel to that end, he must recruit his wondrous helpers. These are men of marked capacity: a fast runner, an infallible marksman, an insatiable eater, an endless drinker, a superhumanly keen hearer, smeller, seer, or whatever else the particular version of the story requires. All such, and more, are to be found at Arthur's court;[1] but their function is usurped by a body of helpers associated with Arthur, some but not all of whom possess the required capacity or quality. Cynddylig the Guide was no worse a guide in the land he had never seen than in his own land; Gwrhyr knew all tongues; Gwalchmei was the best of walkers and the best of riders; Menw could make himself and his

---

[1] See, for example, Henwas the Winged, Huarwar, Long Erwm and Long Atrwm, on p. 73, and Drem, Clust, Huarwar again, and Sugyn, on p. 78.

comrades invisible, and could change his shape, though he was less than a full enchanter of beasts, as his mishap with Twrch Trwyth shows. But some of the tasks postulated by Ysbaddaden and our author require straightforward qualities of resource, cunning, ferocity, and brute strength, and it is in these rather than their itemized wizardry that Cei and Bedwyr show supreme. While for the greatest of the tasks, the hunting of Twrch Trwyth, none will serve but Arthur.

Though Arthur in this story is never styled *ameraudur* (imperator), his men are prophetically solicitous of his dignity. At the beginning of the episode of the Oldest Animals, as at the bloodthirsty but ludicrous attack on the cave of the Black Witch, they are insistent that deeds petty or unseemly are not for Arthur's hand.[1] In the case of the Black Witch he proves them wrong; but he recognizes that it would be a mean exploit to tackle Twrch Trwyth unless he was first assured that he bore the comb and shears between his ears. Even so he is a prompt weapon-wielder and wreaker of deeds. His intervention in the quarrel between Gwyn ap Nudd and Gwythyr is kingly. Incidentally it reveals how one more motif of international folktale, the Unending Battle, has moved within his orbit.

A short while before this Creiddylad daughter of Lludd Silver-hand went with Gwythyr son of Greidawl; and before he had slept with her there came Gwyn son of Nudd and carried her off by force. Gwythyr son of Greidawl gathered a host, and he came to fight with Gwyn son of Nudd. And Gwyn prevailed, and he took prisoner Greid son of Eri, Glinneu son of Taran, and Gwrgwst the Half-naked and Dyfnarth his son. And he took prisoner Pen son of Nethawg, and Nwython, and Cyledyr the Wild his son, and he slew Nwython and took out his heart and compelled Cyledyr to eat his father's heart; and because of this Cyledyr went mad. Arthur heard tell of this, and he came into the North and summoned to him Gwyn son of Nudd and set free his noblemen from his prison, and peace was made between Gwyn son of Nudd and Gwythyr son of Greidawl. This is the peace that was made: the maiden should remain in her father's house, unmolested by either

---

[1] Some *Beowulf* scholars, contemplating their hero's set-to with Grendel's Mother, have been as concerned for Beowulf.

side, and there should be battle between Gwyn and Gwythyr each May-calends for ever and ever, from that day till doomsday; and the one of them that should be victor on doomsday, let him have the maiden (pp. 128–9).

It is remarkable how much of this early British Arthur has survived in the early twelfth-century *Historia Regum Britanniae* of Geoffrey of Monmouth and the mid-fifteenth-century *Morte Darthur* of Sir Thomas Malory. Arthur setting off with Kaius and Bedeuerus to kill the swine-eating, chops-besmeared, rapist giant of St Michael's Mount, and bursting into laughter as the monster crashes to earth like a torn-up oak, or his flaying contest with the beard-collecting Ritho, are cases in point. His development may be traced both backwards and forwards. Behind the royal features in Geoffrey and Malory may be discerned the ruder lineaments of the folk hero; in the folk hero of *Culhwch and Olwen* and the comparable poems may be discovered prefigurations of an imperial countenance.

We may take leave of him with the accomplishment of the final *anoeth*, in which Gwyn and Gwythyr give proof of their reconciliation, Arthur's men give proof of their regard for their lord's dignity, and Arthur gives proof of himself.

Said Arthur, 'Is there any of the marvels still unobtained?' Said one of the men, 'There is: the blood of the Black Witch, daughter of the White Witch, from the head of the Valley of Grief in the uplands of Hell.' Arthur set out for the North and came to where the hag's cave was. And it was the counsel of Gwyn son of Nudd and Gwythyr son of Greidawl that Cacamwri and Hygwydd his brother be sent to fight with the hag. And as they came inside the cave the hag grabbed at them, and caught Hygwydd by the hair of his head and flung him to the floor beneath her. And Cacamwri seized her by the hair of her head, and dragged her to the ground off Hygwydd, but she then turned on Cacamwri and dressed them down both and disarmed them, and drove them out squealing and squalling. And Arthur was angered to see his two servants well nigh slain, and he sought to seize the cave. And then Gwyn and Gwythyr told him, 'It is neither seemly nor pleasant for us to see thee scuffling with a hag. Send Long Amren and Long Eiddil into the cave.' And they went. But if ill was the plight of the first two, the plight of those two was worse, so that God knows not one of the whole four could have stirred from the place, but for the way they were all four loaded on Llamrei, Arthur's mare. And then Arthur seized the entrance to the cave, and from the entrance he took aim at the hag with Carnwennan his knife, and struck her across the middle until she was as two tubs. And Cadw of Prydein took the witch's blood and kept it with him (pp. 135–6).

And so Ysbaddaden, the tasks accomplished, the marvels found, loses his beard, flesh and skin, and his two ears outright. And thereafter his head. 'And that night Culhwch slept with Olwen, and she was his only wife so long as he lived. And the hosts of Arthur dispersed, every one to his country. And in this wise did Culhwch win Olwen daughter of Ysbaddaden Chief Giant.'

4. Hunters with Beasts

FOR NOBLE EFFECTS THE ARTIST NEEDS A NOBLE subject. In Melville's words, in the 103rd chapter of *Moby Dick*: 'To produce a mighty book you must choose a mighty theme. No great and enduring volume can ever be written on the flea, though many there be who have tried it.' So in the active bestiaries of wondertale and legend.

Hunting the Boar is a mighty theme. So is Hunting the Bear and the Whale. Maybe a White Stallion who shakes lightning from his hooves. Assuredly the Lion who carries thunder in his mane. If we see an Assyrian, Persian, or Egyptian monarch portrayed in a hunting scene on fresco, relief, or cylinder seal, he is likely to be transfixing not a flea, or a rabbit, or a squirrel, but a Lion.[1] For Boar, Bear, Whale, and Lion, and all their vasty Peers are heroic and noble beasts who by virtue of their valour, bulk, strength, cunning, and ferocity have impressed themselves on the eye and mind of man, and endlessly challenged his imagination. And challenged it in a firm-set because imposed and conventional way. For example, just as the author of *Culhwch and Olwen* was an assembler and manipulator of folktale patterns, he is himself part of an inescapable narrative pattern of hunt and quest. We have already noticed, when enumerating the tasks associated with the hunting of Twrch Trwyth, that in respect of most of them our author had little freedom of choice.

[1] Not that one has any wish to belittle our ancient fellow-traveller the flea. In a literary way he has served notable comic, satiric, and erotic ends in his time; and socially considered, without him, the louse, the rat, and rheumatism, the Middle Ages would not have known themselves. But though an atom, he is not, in the singular, mighty.

13. CELTIC BOAR FROM NEUVY-EN-SULLIAS

Huntsmen, dogs, horses, weapons, these he must have; a chase
which is processional, by virtue of the dignity of the participants
and the formality and elaboration of the events described; and a
prey part-sacral, because on its prosecution and death depend the
fates of wondertale and legendary protagonists. This straightway
removes most of the hunt and animal literature of our carnivorous
world from present consideration, and fortunately so, if we are not
to be crushed under landslides of the feral slain. Within the established context of story our dealings are not with a boar, but *the*
Boar, not with a whale, but *the* Whale. It is not enough for an essay
in this genre to possess human interest, knowledge of the wild,
literary or historical or documentary importance. We must harden
ourselves, for instance, to set aside folktales, romances, poems, and
fictional records as justly famous as the Arthurian boar-literature of
Sir Gawain and the Green Knight, *Garin de Loherain*, the *Avowynge of
Arther*, and the First Continuation of Chrétien de Troyes' *Perceval*
on the one hand, and the Aesopean bear-literature of Russia
associated with the names of Remizov, Garshin, Krylov, even Pushkin and Tolstoy, on the other. Likewise the boar-hunt in *The
Golden Ass*, though it sufficed for the murder of Lepolemus, the
vengeance and self-immolation of Charites, and the blinding and
incarceration of the love-demented Thrasillus. And likewise the
brief inglorious encounter of man and boar in Book Ten of Ovid's
Metamorphoses, though it sufficed for the death of Adonis and the
birth of the Anemone. So too the two boars, lion, bison, elk, four
aurochs, and grim schelch of the *Nibelungenlied*, and Siegfried's
clowning with his trussed bear; and the hunting of the Magic Pig
by the Fianna in *Duanaire Finn*, where the slaughter of thirty warriors,
nine attendants, and one hundred and forty dogs, together with
some very fine knife-work by the unspillable Colla, is still not
enough. It is with the Irish and Scottish tales of Diarmaid and the
Boar of Beann-Gulbain which in conjunction with the perfidy of
Finn brought Diarmaid to his death that we come within range of
the full power and dignity of our chosen theme. If we were looking
for powerful but fictional examinations of human nature in a context
of bear or lion we need look no further than Selma Lagerlöf, Marten
Hansen, and Ernest Hemingway. 'Vor Frues Jaeger' and 'The Short

14. A WELSH HUNTSMAN
From Llangan

Happy Life of Francis Macomber' are splendid of their kind, but in our present context it is the wrong kind of kind. If for a self-searching no less compelling and this time factual, who could ask for more than Knud Rasmussen's 'The Bear in the Ice Hole'—a man of action's spare account of a true adventure which is also a parable for mankind, humorous, clear-sighted, cruel, and wry—but in our present context the wrong kind of parable.

To touch on the excellence of just two of these variations on a theme of Man-kills-Beast: the brawned and bristled sengler of *Sir Gawain* is indeed a noble boar of this world, a snapper of dogs' backbones and up-ender of men; and Sir Bertilak de Hautdesert is indeed a noble knight of this world, courteous, masterful, and of an unflinching valour. And never was there a sterner moment of truth when with the boar at bay, the froth foaming hideously at the corners of his mouth and his white tusks clashing, the knight dismounts, plucks out his bright sword, and wades the stream against him.

The beast was aware of the man with his weapon in hand. He set his hairs a-bristling, snorted so fiercely that many were afraid for the man, lest he get the worse of it. The boar came rushing out straight at the knight, so that man and boar were in heaps in the fiercest of the water. But the other had the worse, for the man marks him well when first they encountered, set his point firmly right in his breast-hollow and hit him up to the hilt, so that the heart split open, and he gave up his life snarling and went swiftly downstream (1586-96).

A true English beast this, thick in the arm and thick in the head, without the sense to know when he is beaten. In a similar sort of way the bears of Pushkin and Garshin are true nineteenth-century Russians, for the most part in chains, and for the most part unhappy. Not so the boar of Beann-Gulbain, though his story in the Irish version might appear to invite pity. He had begun his mortal course as the son of the steward of Angus, the fosterer of Diarmaid son of Duibhne. In a jealous fit Duibhne squeezed the steward's son between his knees and killed him. The steward, denied price or vengeance for his dead son, struck the body with his wand and turned him into a huge wild boar, without ears or tail, declaring that

Diarmaid and the boar should have the same span of life and at last kill each other. Long years afterwards, when Finn and Diarmaid were nominally reconciled after their irreconcilable feud, this was the boar which so ravaged the Fianna that neither man nor dog could make stand against him. Diarmaid hears the yelping of a hound in the night, and goes to investigate, but not with his big sword, the Moralltach, and his big spear, the Ga-dearg (Big Fury and Red Javelin), but with his lesser sword, the Beag-alltach, and his lesser spear, the Ga-buidhe (Little Fury and Yellow Javelin). He meets Finn on the summit of Beann-Gulbain, and for the first time hears of the *geis*, the prohibition laid on him, that he must never hunt a wild boar lest he meet his own death. But hero that he was, and for all his misgivings, he awaits the boar's onset, as Finn knew he would. First his dog fails him, then his light spear, and finally his swordblade. The boar dashes off with him, then throws him to the ground and cruelly ranches his side, but Diarmaid uses the sword-hilt as a missile and strikes him to the brain, so that he falls lifeless. Finn arrives with his followers the Fianna, and full prey to the bitterness of the past, rejoices to see his bright-faced enemy Diarmaid-of-the-Women, who had carried off his bride Gráinne, lying there pale and mangled. Diarmaid, as a return for his services to Finn, asks for a drink of water from between Finn's palms, which had the property of healing all sickness and wounds. Finn's answer was a cold one, twice-repeated, but at the urging of Oscar he consents to fetch water from the nearby well. But twice he opened his palms and the water ran away, and as he fetched it the third time Diarmaid expired.[1]

If now we ask ourselves why Sir Bertilak's calamitous boar with his gnashing tusks, or Rasmussen's yellow bear with his jingling icicles, and Hansen's colossal slagbjørn holed up by the altar of the deserted church in Ådalen, are not fit quarry for the Great Hunt, which is the heart of our Mighty Theme, the answer is that for all

[1] S. H. O'Grady (ed.), *The Pursuit after Diarmaid O'Duibhne and Grainne*, Dublin, for the Ossianic Society, 1857. In the so-called 'Lay of Diarmaid' and the prose 'Diarmaid and Gráinne', both orally collected for J. F. Campbell's *Popular Tales of the West Highlands*, the boar has a sixteen-foot rigbone but is not more than a boar.

their magnificence as animals each is himself and nothing more than that self. They are all that tooth and claw, muscle and hide can make them, dowered with the will to live, and the cunning and ferocity to enforce it. But each is immediately destructible by the weapons of men. In their nature they are animal, mortal, and apprehended as such. Not so *Culhwch and Olwen*'s Twrch Trwyth and the Calydonian Boar of Book Eight of Ovid's *Metamorphoses*, ancients both, or the titular beasts of Melville's *Moby Dick* and Faulkner's *The Bear*, which serve as their modern counterparts. Twrch Trwyth, we have seen, terrifying as he is in bulk and valour, is not merely a boar. He is a king whom God transformed into that shape for his sins, unreconciled and unreconcilable, his temper rancorous, his moods inhumane, his royal intelligence undimmed by his beast vision.

Ovid's boar has been loosed on Calydonia by the goddess Diana to punish its people for neglecting her sacrifice:

> Wrath touches ev'n the Gods; the Queen of Night
> Fir'd with Disdain, and jealous of her Right,
> Unhonour'd though I am, at least, said she,
> Not unreveng'd that impious Act shall be.
> Swift as the Word, she sped the Boar away,
> With Charge on those devoted Fields to prey.

By size and armament he was stupendously equipped to do so: as Ovid, metamorphoséd by Dryden, shows:

> No larger Bulls th'*Ægyptian* Pastures feed,
> And none so large *Sicilian* Meadows breed:
> His Eye-balls glare with Fire suffus'd with Blood;
> His Neck shoots up a thick-set thorny Wood;
> His bristled Back a Trench impal'd appears,
> And stands erected, like a Field of Spears.
> Froth fills his Chaps, he sends a grunting Sound,
> And part he churns, and part befoams the Ground.
> For Tusks with *Indian* Elephants he strove,
> And *Jove's* own Thunder from his Mouth he drove.

Melville's whale is Moby Dick, the White Whale, ubiquitous and immortal, known through long ages and in many seas, wise, treacherous, vengeful, unique in mass and colour, the baffler and mangler of those that would destroy him. Moreover admitted into all the 'rights, privileges, and distinctions of a name . . . as much a name as Cambyses or Caesar.' And in this, one of the 'plainest and most palpable wonders of the world.'

Was it not so, O Timor Tom! thou famed leviathan, scarred like an iceberg, who so long didst lurk in the Oriental straits of that name, whose spout was oft seen from the palmy beach of Ombay? Was it not so, O New Zealand Jack! thou terror of all cruisers that crossed their wakes in the vicinity of the Tattoo Land? Was it not so, O Morquan! King of Japan, whose lofty jet they say at times assumed the semblance of a snow-white cross against the sky? Was it not so, O Don Miguel! thou Chilian whale, marked like an old tortoise with mystic hieroglyphs upon the back?

Such witness stays not to be questioned, and if overtaken would prove rebuttive. And so with Faulkner's bear, Old Ben, spirit and lord of the Wilderness,

an anachronism indomitable and invincible out of an old dead time, a phantom, epitome and apotheosis of the old wild life which the little puny humans swarmed and hacked at in a fury of abhorrence and fear like pygmies about the ankles of a drowsing elephant—the old bear, solitary, indomitable, and alone; widowered, childless, and absolved of mortality—old Priam reft of his old wife and outlived all his sons.

He too had earned a name. 'Old Ben, the two-toed bear in a land where bears with trap-ruined feet had been called Two-Toe or Three-Toe or Cripple-Foot for fifty years, only Old Ben was an extra bear (the head bear, General Compson called him) and so had earned a name such as a human man could have worn and not been sorry.' Not a bear, not a whale, nor boars, entirely of this world. There is a sacral element in their hunting, what Faulkner calls 'the yearly pageant-rite of the old bear's furious immortality'. Their lives are touched with the supernatural and their deaths challenge eschatology. And further to Old Ben—it must be with a considerable sense of recognition that Welsh readers of *Culhwch and Olwen* read these sentences concerning him. Sam Fathers and young McCaslin have heard the Bear walking through the woods, with the frightened yapping dogs for chorus. Not running. Walking.

"He do it every year," Sam said. "Ash and Boon say he comes up here to run the other little bears away. Tell them to get to hell out of here and stay out until the hunters are gone. . . . *He don't care no more for bears than he does for gods or men neither.* He come to see who's here, who's new in camp this year, whether he can shoot or not, can stay or not. *Whether we got the dog yet that can bay him and hold him* until a man gets there with a gun. Because he's *the head bear.*"

As Ysgithyrwyn in *Culhwch and Olwen* was head boar (or more literally head, chief, of boars, *penbeidd*), and a curious doublet of the royal boar Twrch Trwyth.[1]

[1] It would be an extensive task to discuss the role of even one of these beasts in religion, worship, mythology, magic, superstition, legend, wondertale, and folklore, so that we might fully appreciate its fitness to be a heroic quarry—quite apart from the circumstance that its natural attributes make it a quarry for heroes. Thus the boar appears frequently and significantly in the Bronze Age rock-engravings (*hällristningar*) of Scandinavia, and not infrequently but significantly in Celtic sculpture in stone and metal in Central Europe, the Iberian Peninsula and Gaul, not, one assumes, as boar-god, but as the visual image of a god or as a sacral beast associated with a god through character-istics of its own. His procreative power appealed to agricultural peoples; he was associated as a cult animal with the fertility god Frey in Germania, with Tanaris and Teutates in Gaul, and with Celtic and Germanic funerary practice. He was closely connected with Celtic Otherworld story, for ex-ample in the Third and Fourth Branches of the Mabinogi. His strength, ferocity, and valour won him the regard of warriors; his effigy was at once menacing and protective, as witness *Beowulf* 303-6, the Sutton Hoo, Vendel, and Benty Grange helmets, pictured runestones, and the decorative plates of Torslunda. A man could be named Boar (Eofor, Galti), and the fury of a brave man in battle be likened to the wild boar's fury, from Bleiddyn and Caradawg of the *Gododdin* who perished at Catraeth, and the frenzied hero of 'The Stanzas of the Graves' who 'whilst he slew thee he would smile at thee', to the English Alfred who, as Asser records, led his men like a wild boar against the vikings at Ashdown.

In *Thithreks Saga* the killing of Sigurd is ascribed by the terrible Hogni to a wild boar, as though he of all animals was most capable of so prime a quell; and in the *Nibelungenlied* it was Kriemhild's ill-omened dream concerning Siegfried that 'two boars chased him over the heath and the flowers were dyed with blood.' There was an early link between boar and sword: his flesh was

The destruction of these supernatural or part-supernatural beasts is the task, duty, and pleasure of the chosen of the land. Chosen for merit, and no less by destiny. In Ovid's phrase (but Dryden's words): 'The Chiefs their honourable Danger sought.' For the Aper Calydonius, Meleager and Atalanta; Jason, Theseus, Perithous; Nestor then but young; Laertes active and Ancaeus bold; Mopsus the sage who future things foretold. With these fair Leda's sons, Achilles' father, and 'a thousand others of immortal Fame'. For Twrch Trwyth, and here one mighty theme meets another, Arthur and his hosts. For Moby Dick the ship's crew of the *Pequod*, none fished from the shoal of ordinary men, Captain Ahab of the riven brow and ivory leg; Queequeg the purplish-yellow, bald and scalp-locked, tooth-filed idol worshipper, head-pedlar and cannibal, son of a king, native of Kokovoko, that faraway island not shown on any map ('true places never are'); Tashtego the Red Indian; Daggoo the black man and Fedallah the yellow; the tortured, valour-ruined mate Tarbuck, Little Pip, the Old Manx Sailor with his dream of death, and Ishmael the otherwise nameless, sole survivor of the hunt. In Ahab's order of battle these and their like were the captains of companies, knights and squires, and assigned as such. For Old Ben must be assembled famed hunters and haunters of the wilderness: Major de Spain and General Compson, McCaslin and Walter Ewell, the flat report of whose rifle spoke death to every quarry; young McCaslin, the boy, the 'he', the grower-up; Boon Hogganbeck and Tennie's Jim, their histories spelled to us in a

---

traditionally the food of heroes, providing those prestigious and dangerous pork-eaters the Celts with the Champion's Portion (*curad-mir*) in this world, and the entire meat of Odinn's *einherjar* in the next. In oath-taking, we are informed, the back of the *sonargöltr*, the atonement– or sacrifice-boar, was binding as an altar. And finally the Three Mighty Swineherds of the Island of Britain were beings no less august than Pryderi, prince of Dyfed and son of Pwyll Head of Annwn; Drystan (Tristan) who minded the swine of March (Mark) son of Meirchion while their true keeper bore a message to Esyllt, and defended them so successfully against Arthur, March, Cei, and Bedwyr, that they seized never a pig, neither by guile, by force, nor by stealing; and Coll son of Collfrewi, who in one of the most sensational entries in the annals of pigdom stayed with the sow Henwen (Old White) from Cornwall to Arfon, and so brought wheat, barley, and bees, to say nothing of Palug's Cat, to our western parts.

score of books and stories; and Sam Fathers, part white, part black, part redskin, descendant of kings and slaves, who knew his own death, like Boon's tenuous reason, entwined with that of the bear he hunted.

These then are the hunters, the legendary or heroic assemblages. Not men who hunt for meat alone (as Rasmussen), for the pleasures of the chase (as Sir Bertilak—who admittedly has a further aim in view), or to define the ethics of the kill (so Hemingway's Wilson and the Macombers), and least of all for a practical joke (as with Sieg-fried's bear set free in the kitchen). The hunting of Twrch Trwyth is an enjoined task, and the fulfilment of a royal oath which unful-filled must cost Arthur his honour. The Aper Calydonius threatens the ruin of a race and the wreck of a countryside; it is the fair task of heroes to contain such destruction by destroying its author. For the undoing of Moby Dick (if indeed he is undone) we need the monomania of the dismasted Ahab, whose days are a paean of hatred and his nights a dream of revenge. 'Swim away from me, do ye?' And the mutter rising to a lion's roar: 'Up helm! Keep her off round the world!' On the altar of this satanic ambition he offers up com-fort, love, family, decency, all peace of mind, makes sacrifice of his ship, his crew, and his life. On one level he is an inexhaustible repository of lore, skill, and practice, on another the professor of an idiocy malignant and sublime. He is a man possessed, driven by his daemon, lost to this world. None other could hope to match the lore and skill and daemon of the White Whale. The hunters of Old Ben are likewise victims of an obsession. What is true of young McCaslin has been true of them all.

It ran in his knowledge before he ever saw it. It loomed and towered in his dreams before he even saw the unaxed woods where it left its crooked print, shaggy, tremendous, red-eyed, not malevolent, but just big, too big for the dogs which tried to bay it, for the horses which tried to ride it down, for the men and the bullets they fired into it; too big for the very country which was its constricting scope.

Old Ben was not only head bear, he was the wilderness itself which these men loved and timelessly pursued and sought so to immerse themselves in that they would be possessed by and of it for ever. They are in fact pursuing the end of their world; the yearly pageant-rite, the annual race of destroyed and destroyers (all destroyers, and all to be destroyed), avert nothing. And when at last they kill Old Ben (and Old Ben kills Lion) the catastrophe is upon them, not fast and heavy as a felled beech, but as a tired elm sighs and groans and withers, feels rot and canker in branch and bole, shrinks in the root, is fretted to defeat. Sam Fathers, with whom young McCaslin saw the phantom buck which the old man called Chief and Grandfather, ceased from living; Boon's wits addled; the lumbermen move in; the free hunters prepare to degenerate into a club; an alphabet of Wilderness contracts to a delta. We have lived through the ritual, and what remains grows meaningless—or has meaning in a new and dreadful way: we are heading, in *Go Down, Moses*, from the clean-killed bear and sacrificial son of three peoples towards a murdered policeman and an electrocuted negro in Chicago.

So much, if so little, of the men. 'Now, Muse, let's sing of Dogs.' Ovid's Muse sings but briefly. Of the collected heroes, 'Some from the Chains the faithful Dogs unbound', which is all we hear of them till the Boar is in their midst:

> The Beast impetuous with his Tusks aside
> Deals glancing Wounds; the fearful Dogs divide:
> All spend their Mouth aloof, but none abide.

The only one to get a separate mention is the unfortunate creature killed, so maladroitly, by Jason:

> Once more bold Jason threw, but failed to wound
> The Boar, and slew an undeserving Hound;
> And through the Dog the Dart was nailed to Ground.

It would be wrong for a nation of dog-lovers to conclude that for such misdemeanour the Argonauts' high admiral should be broken to third mate; but it was a *bêtise* which the killers of Old Ben took pains to avoid. We may conclude that in Calydonia a wise dog was a dog who knew his right place.

For even the wisest dogs in *Culhwch and Olwen* this was a hard place to know. The Catalogue of Tasks requires that Drudwyn be found, the whelp of Greid son of Eri. Thereafter we hear that only a leash made from the beard of Dillus the Bearded can hold 'those two whelps', and this held by a huntsman nine times wilder than the wild beast on the mountain. Also, 'Twrch Trwyth will never be hunted until Aned and Aethlem be obtained. Swift as a gust of wind would they be; never were they unleashed on a beast they did not kill.' And finally there is mention of the three dogs of Bwlch, Cyfwlch, and Syfwlch: by name, we think, Glas, Glesig, Gleisad. But in the accomplishment of the tasks the dogs are heavily confused. Arthur, without explanation, sets off to secure the two whelps of the bitch Rhymhi who in the shape of a she-wolf is destroying stock in Aber Cleddyf. Before the attack on Ysgithyrwyn Chief Boar he had gone to Ireland to secure the two dogs of Glythfyr Ledewig. To add to our troubles, the Ysgithyrwyn episode concludes with the inexplicable words, 'It was not the dogs which Ysbaddaden had named to Culhwch which killed the boar, but Cafall, Arthur's own dog.' The assault on Twrch Trwyth and his brood was launched with 'all the dogs that had been named to this end.' The canine heroes of the hunt, we have seen, and will see again, are Aned and Aethlem.

And so it is with Old Ben. There too the bear's death will not be achieved till the right dogs are found. 'We aint got the dog yet', said Sam Fathers. 'It won't take but one. But he aint there. Maybe he aint nowhere.' In fact there are three dogs, a brave little bitch who just has to prove that she's brave, and a dog young McCaslin had at home, 'a mongrel, of the sort called fyce by negroes, a ratter, itself not much bigger than a rat and possessing that sort of courage which had long since stopped being bravery and had become foolhardiness'; and finally the dog named Lion, yellow-eyed, lion-chested, and all over the colour of a blued gun-barrel, like Old Ben a creature of the Wilderness, like Rhymhi a killer of calves and foals, subjected (but not tamed) by Sam Fathers; a dog so strong, so fearless, so hate-filled, that to Boon it seemed for a time easier to catch the bear and use him to hunt the dog than tame the dog and use him to hunt the bear. A dog who in *Mabinogion* phrase (and Sam Fathers') 'would never cry on a trail'. A dog who didn't need a nose, for as Sam Fathers said, 'All he need is a bear.'

Also horses. In Ovid unsung. In *Culhwch and Olwen* Gwyn Dunmane, the white steed of Mabon, and Du, the black steed of Gwyn son of Nudd; Arthur's Llamrei, and the unnamed mount of Cyledyr the Wild. In *The Bear* General Compson's horse who couldn't quite face it, and the unblenching one-eyed mule Katie. In *Moby Dick* for dogs and horses we must make do with boats.

And weapons. No surprises here. In Ovid the expected armoury of spears, swords, at least one axe, and the bow and arrows proper to the virgin huntress Atalanta. In *Culhwch and Olwen* such resplendent war-gear as befits famous men: of Bwlch and his notchy brothers, we are informed, three gleaming glitterers their three shields, three pointed piercers their three spears, three keen carvers their three swords; in Culhwch's one hand two whetted spears of silver, in his other a battle-axe whose length from ridge to edge was the length of a man's forearm, and so sharp that it would draw blood from the wind; on his thigh a gold-hilted sword, and slung behind him a shield decorated with gold and elephant ivory. The head of the one-handed Bedwyr's spear would leave its shaft, draw blood from the wind, and settle upon the shaft again. The wondrous qualities of Wrnach's sword, so horribly obtained, are not mentioned, nor does it play a named part in the hunt; but the knife of Osla Big-knife merits attention. It was short (comparatively so, one would judge) and broad, and when Arthur and his hosts came to a torrent's edge, a narrow place on the water would be sought, and his knife in its sheath laid across the torrent, and that would be bridge enough for the hosts of the Three Realms of Britain and its three adjacent islands with their spoil. That he should carry it into the Severn in pursuit of Twrch Trwyth is understandable; that when its sheath filled with water he almost drowned was inevitable; but what shall we say of Cacamwri and the two quernstones that almost drowned *him* (see p. 90 above)?

The Bear is not without its oddities. Not the shotguns and rifles which failed even to bleed Old Ben—they are commonplace enough —or the worn and blueless guns of the swampers and patch-farmers assembled for the kill; but Walter Ewell's flat-sounding death-knell

of a rifle, and the ridiculous pump-gun of Boon, who once missed the
Bear five times at twenty-five feet, and indeed never hit anything
in his life except a plate-glass window and a negro woman's leg or
bottom. It was a knife, not a gun, with which he would single-
handed, he and Lion, reach Old Ben's mortal nerve, and despatch
his own sanity. In *Moby Dick* we have, in addition to the normal
brutal ironmongery of the whaler, Queequeg's fearsome harpoon
(delicate enough to shave with, but grim to rend Behemoth), and
the harpoon forged aboard ship for Ahab from the gathered nail-
stubbs of the steel shoes of racing-horses—its barbs fashioned from
Ahab's razors, tempered not in thin water but in the thick donated
blood of Tashtego, Queequeg, Daggoo, and baptized not in the
name of the Father but *in nomine diaboli*.

And here, at this point of time, as Ahab's malignant iron devours
the baptismal blood, and we wait on summation in Calydon, Yok-
napatawpha, Ynys Prydein, and the Japanese Sea, it will be well to
make clear that in bringing these four works of literature into
common focus, nothing cries out to be proved. There is a river in
Culhwch and Olwen and a river in *The Bear*; and Twrch Trwyth is
headed into the one and gets out of it, and Old Ben heads into the
other and gets out of it. But I should be almost as surprised to learn
that Faulkner, folktale-bibber though he was, had read *Culhwch and
Olwen* as that the Welshman had read *The Bear*. We can be confident
that Ovid had read neither, and while Melville's field of reference
(supplied by a Sub-Sub-Librarian) stretches from Job and Jonah to
Plutarch and Pliny, and from Octher or Other to Coffin and Cook, it
does not stretch to Roman or Welshman and cannot reach the
Yoknapatawphan. Primarily we should think of these works, or in
the case of the *Metamorphoses* and *Culhwch and Olwen* the relevant
portions of these works, as independent essays on a Mighty Theme
for whom correspondences are inevitable.

For Ovid the hunting of the Calydonian Boar was the necessary
prelude to the destruction of Meleager by his mother Althaea, to
avenge the death of her brothers at his hand. For the Welshman the
hunting of Twrch Trwyth is one of the tasks laid on Culhwch by
Ysbaddaden, which must be accomplished before he can wed his
bride, the Giant's Daughter. Both are short and stylized exercises.

Moby Dick is a vast novel in every respect: awesome in size, scope, style, faults, conception, and in achievement—one of the world's great novels. It is, of course, more than we have even hinted at yet: in a loose and modern sense a theological work, its author at grips with the insoluble problems of existence and destiny, the compulsive universe, and the defiant gestures, at once vain and heroic, of the helplessly struggling individual. *The Bear* is one short story in a collection of short stories—a very long short story, true, too long, true, filled with compassion and wonder and the genius of place as well as with moving incidents and characters—and with a deep and painful wisdom. One of the New World's great short stories. And Faulkner, like Melville: 'One—but a Lion!' Both are primitive and heroic authors, re-creators of wondertale and legend, searchers for a linking meaning in the lives of all nature's creatures, and would-be comprehenders of cosmic truth; and their books are vast half-apprehended continents to whose deserts, forests, oceans, and mountain ranges we are for ever forced to return on a quest of our own. It would be an incursion into folly to argue for sources, influences, analogues, consequences, borrowings, deviations. Our business is rather to observe how the common theme—the hunting of a great beast not wholly of this world—makes common demands on who would handle it.

Even minor correspondences will not be sought in vain. The footprint, one of the marvels of Britain, left by Arthur's dog Cafall when he was hunting the boar Troit (or Troynt, see p. 87), is at once too frequent a motif in folktale and saint's legend, and too atmospheric a device of the novelist to fall into disuse. Just so young McCaslin, 'standing beside Sam in the thick great gloom of ancient woods and the winter's dying afternoon, looked quietly down at the rotted log scored and gutted with claw-marks and, in the wet earth beside it, the print of the enormous warped two-toed foot.' There is Arthur's moment of bitter resolution: 'Twrch Trwyth has slain many of my men. Not while I am alive shall he go into Cornwall. I will pursue him no further, but I will join with him life for life.' And Major de Spain (mistakenly, as it happens): 'He has killed mine and McCaslin's dogs, but that was all right. We gambled the dogs against him; we gave each other warning. But now he has

come into my house and destroyed my property, out of season too.'
That two such dedicated slaughterers expect boar and bear to keep
their punches up and retire to their corners at the sound of the bell
requires no documentation from folktale: it accords with the enduring principle of human self-importance, and will be found anywhere
at any time in man's portentous history.

But it is time to look to the hunt's end. A bloody, spumy death
took off the Otherworld Boar of classical legend, the Aper Calydonius. After a brave ripping and rending of heroes, Meleager's
point reached his brawn-shielded heart. Not Diana herself could
save him.

The Bear too had to die. He had survived fifty-two bullet wounds,
buckshot, rifle, and ball (O fifty tridents of the Salmon of Llyn
Llyw, and the uncounted battle scars of the White Whale), and
would die now of a dog, a knife, and a man.

This time the bear didn't strike him down. It caught the dog in
both arms, almost loverlike, and they both went down. The boy was
off the mule now. He drew back both hammers of the gun but he
could see nothing but moiling spotted houndbodies until the bear
surged up again. Boon was yelling something, he could not tell what;
he could see Lion still clinging to the bear's throat and he saw the
bear, half erect, strike one of the hounds with one paw and hurl it five
or six feet and then, rising and rising as though it would never stop,
stand erect again and begin to rake at Lion's belly with its forepaws.
Then Boon was running. The boy saw the gleam of the blade in his
hand and watched him leap among the hounds, hurdling them, kick-
ing them aside as he ran, and fling himself astride the bear as he had
hurled himself on to the mule, his legs locked around the bear's belly,
his left arm under the bear's throat where Lion clung, and the glint
of the knife as it rose and fell.

It fell just once. For an instant they almost resembled a piece of
statuary: the clinging dog, the bear, the man astride its back, working and probing the buried blade. Then they went down, pulled over
backward by Boon's weight, Boon underneath. It was the bear's back
which reappeared first but at once Boon was astride it again. He had
never released the knife and again the boy saw the almost infinitesimal
movement of his arm and shoulder as he probed and sought; then the
bear surged erect, raising with it the man and the dog too, and

turned and still carrying the man and the dog it took two or three steps toward the woods on its hind feet as a man would have walked and crashed down. It didn't collapse, crumple. It fell all of a piece, as a tree falls, so that all three of them, man, dog, and bear, seemed to bounce once.

And our own Twrch Trwyth, we know what happened to him. Or do we? 'And then he was forced out of Cornwall and driven straight forward into the sea. From that time forth never a one has known where he went, and Aned and Aethlem with him.' Did Twrch Trwyth and the two pursuing dogs reach some happy apple-orchard in the west? Alas, one fears that the grim old warrior, dis-kingdomed and unchilded, found briny sepulchre for his smarting wounds. Or are the two things one, and by land- or water-gate he regained the Otherworld? Aned and Aethlem, who were never un-leashed on a beast they did not kill, for them there is little hope: they were of Lion's breed, and could not survive their quarry. But for Twrch Trwyth, when one contemplates as a wise man will, from Tintagel or Land's End, the three diminishing arrow-heads on the gold-fallow water, the thing is not finished, the wondertale chance remains.

Likewise the White Whale. What became of Morquan's peer, him of the lofty jet and foaming wake, after that last and fatal three-day battle in shark-infested waters, Ragnarok of the *Pequod* and her fated crew? The battle which has the destruction of the two mates' boats, and the huge beast Leviathan, maddened by the harpoons and irons suppurating in him, smiting the *Pequod*'s star-board with the solid white buttress of his forehead till she was breached and—'The ship? Great God, where is the ship?'

In respect of Ahab we are in no doubt. First his desperate talk of omen and riddle after the disasters of the second day's battle: 'This whole act's immutably decreed. 'Twas rehearsed by thee and me a billion years before this ocean rolled. Fool! I am the Fates' lieuten-ant; I act under orders.' And later: 'The things called omens. . . . There's a riddle now might baffle all the lawyers backed by the ghosts of the whole line of judges—like a hawk's beak it pecks my brain. *I'll, I'll* solve it, though!' And so we reach his last gesture of unquenchable and suicidal hate.

The harpoon was darted; the stricken whale flew forward, with igniting velocity the line ran through the groove; ran foul. Ahab stooped to clear it; he did clear it; but the flying turn caught him round the neck, and voicelessly as Turkish mutes bowstring their victim, he was shot out of the boat. Next instant, the heavy eye-splice in the rope's final end flew out of the stark-empty tub, knocked down an oarsman, and smiting the sea, disappeared in its depths.

Did then the White Whale, his hunter dead behind him, surge on to gird the world's round ball, now off Japan, now off Greenland, now like Don Miguel sounding by the Chilean coast? Or like Twrch Trwyth, if that was the Boar's demission, with a wake of blood and foam, did he plough the main to the ebbing of his strength, and then, his flanks gashed and corroded by the hooks and killing-irons of man, and the beaks and jaw-grids of his sea-predators, roll, bloat, and whelm, then vanish for ever in the blue sarcophagus of ocean?

'To produce a mighty book you must choose a mighty theme.' Here are the last words of the novel *Moby Dick*. (We pause only to recall that white-tailed, grey-headed veteran of seashores, our British star-pecker and salmon-leech, the Eagle of Gwernabwy.) The *Pequod*'s deck and works have vanished in the vortex. Only the tip of her mainmast may be discerned, that mainmast to which the Indian Tashtego had been nailing Ahab's red flag of defiance.

But as the last whelmings intermixingly poured themselves over the sunken head of the Indian at the mainmast, leaving a few inches of the erect spar yet visible, together with long streaming yards of the flag, which calmly undulated, with ironical coincidings, over the destroying billows they almost touched;—at that instant, a red arm and a hammer hovered backwardly uplifted in the open air, in the act of nailing the flag faster and yet faster to the subsiding spar. A sky-hawk that tauntingly had followed the main-truck downwards from its natural home among the stars, pecking at the flag, and incommoding Tashtego there; this bird now chanced to intercept its broad fluttering wing between the hammer and the wood; and simultaneously feeling that ethereal thrill, the submerged savage beneath, in his death-gasp, kept his hammer frozen there; and so the bird of heaven, with archangelic shrieks, and his imperial beak thrust upwards, and his whole captive form folded in the flag of Ahab, went down with his ship, which, like Satan, would not sink to hell till she had dragged a living part of heaven along with her, and helmeted herself with it.

Now small fowls flew screaming over the yet yawning gulf; a sullen white surf beat against its steep sides; then all collapsed, and the great shroud of the sea rolled on as it rolled five thousand years ago.

III. KING HROLF'S SAGA

1. The Bear's Son

KING HROLF'S SAGA OR THE SAGA OF HROLF KRAKI (HRÓLFS
Saga Kraka) is one of the best known and most highly prized of the
Fornaldar Sögur, those Sagas of Olden Times which constitute one
of the three categories of Icelandic saga-telling most familiar to
English-language readers, whose indicatory characteristics are as
follows.[1]

First, there are the historical sagas, or Kings' Lives. The best
known of these and the most easily available to English readers is
Snorri Sturluson's Heimskringla, or Lives of the Kings of Norway, a
superb and consummatory work of c. 1230–35, but there had been
much admirable historical biography written, and bishops' lives too,
from as early as the second half of the twelfth century. The authors
of the Kings' Lives would in good faith have described themselves
as seekers after truth, and such for the most part they were, though
their notion of historical truth, as of history, was different from ours.
Political and economic causation meant less to them than the clash
of personalities; they were innocent of statistics but strong on
argument and narrative; and they considered it not merely their
right but their duty to fill in all such hiatuses in the chronological

[1] The traditional classification of the Icelandic sagas has been in six categories,
the remaining three being, (a) Bishops' Sagas, (b) Sturlunga Saga and other
sagas relating to Iceland in the twelfth and thirteenth centuries, and (c) the
Fornsögur or Riddara Sögur, versions of southern knightly romance. These I
have omitted as not relevant to my purpose. For other proposed classifications
see Sigurður Nordal, Sagalitteraturen (Nordisk Kultur, 1953), and Hermann
Pálsson, 'Um eðli Íslendingasagna' (Skírnir, 1969; likewise Hermann Pálsson
and Paul Edwards, Legendary Fiction in Medieval Iceland, Studia Islandica 30,
Reykjavík, 1971).

record as they could not furnish out from their oral and written sources. This last was an easier task for the centuries after the achievements of Harald Bluetooth in Denmark and Harald Fairhair in Norway, and the colonization of Iceland from *c.* 870, than it could ever be for that obscure sixth century to which we ascribe the one verifiable historical event in *Beowulf* (Hygelac's fatal raid on Frisia) and the legendary history of persons and dynasties plentiful in that poem and luxuriant in *Hrólfs Saga Kraka.* Thus Snorri's introductory saga in his *Heimskringla*, the *Ynglinga Saga*, which carries the royal pedigrees of the North back to Yngvi-Frey, 'God of the World and Sovereign of the Swedes', shares much of its subject matter with the *Fornaldar Sögur*, but as *Ynglinga Saga* progresses its author concerns himself increasingly with fact, sometimes true, sometimes mistaken, and where that is missing with the probable or at least plausible reconstruction of fact, and where even that defies him, with skilled and reasonable invention. This difference of aim and method is fundamental between King's Life and Saga of Olden Times.

Second we distinguish the Sagas of Icelanders. The authors of the Kings' Lives had no choice but to look abroad, most of all to Norway, and there most of all to the two Olafs, Olaf Tryggvason and Olaf the Saint. But the authors of the *Íslendinga Sögur* found most of their subject matter at home, and their hundred and more sagas, short or long, provide us with a domestic history of their fellow-countrymen during most of the tenth and the first third of the eleventh centuries, as this was revealed through the lives of outstanding men and the traditions of important families. This again was not history or even biography in the modern sense. Rather it was historical or biographical tradition ranging from the near factual to the wholly fictitious, so greatly was it affected by the creative imagination of story-tellers, authors, and scribes, by the changes to which oral tradition is subjected over a period of two to three hundred years, and the distortions inevitable when men of antiquarian interests and family pride portray one age partly in terms of another. It was a notably incomplete tradition, in that it was largely concerned with feud and violence. Quiet days and peaceful years were sacrificed to times of action, with their harsh preliminaries and harsher consequences. It follows that the family sagas are both more and less than history. The best, indeed the majority, of them, rest on a foundation of history and antiquarian speculation; but it was history seen in terms of men and women and human destiny, and in form of a shaped story. A saga was not the fixed and immutable record of known facts. It was an individual's version and interpretation of facts, and could undergo shortening, lengthening, interpolation of new material, deliberate change, accidental manipulation, misunderstanding, and invention. No generalization is without its perils, but the great sagas are most properly to be regarded as creative literature not history, which is why, when we consider them as examinations of human conduct within the conventions of prose narrative distinct from chronicle or annal, the sagas that tell of Njall, Egill, and Grettir, to name three masterpieces only, have no parallels in medieval literature and appear like mighty foreshadowings of the European novel.

If we accept as broad and qualifiable truths that the primary aims of the Icelandic historians from Ari Thorgilsson (1067–1148) to Snorri Sturluson (1179–1241) were to preserve and instruct, and of the authors of the Sagas of Icelanders in the thirteenth century to instruct and entertain, we shall not be wide of the mark if we classify the main business of the authors of the Sagas of Olden Times as to entertain. As the author, editor, or scribe of *Göngu-Hrólfs Saga* advises us: 'Since neither this nor any other thing can be made to please everybody, no one need believe any more of it than he wants to believe; but it is always the best and most profitable thing to listen while a story is being told, and get pleasure from it, and not be gloomy.' The historian hoped to be judged truthful, and the sagaman to appear truthful, but the hopes of the writer of a legendary saga lay elsewhere. 'Whether this is true or not', we are instructed at the end of *Hrólfs Saga Gautrekssonar*, 'let those who can enjoy the story; but those who can't had better find some other amusement.'[1] The Sagas of Olden Times were in large measure retold and protectively coloured wondertale, and even when in the guise of hero-tale they abut on history, geography, real persons,

[1] This and the preceding quotation are taken from Pálsson and Edwards, *Legendary Fiction in Medieval Iceland*, p. 21. See too Hermann Pálsson, *Sagnaskemmtun Íslendinga*, Reykjavík, 1962.

and traditional events, the wondrous still dominates. The materials from which they were assembled are readily identifiable: the corpus of popular wondertale as it was known in the Scandinavian homelands; the corpus of myth and legend relating to the pagan deities and the creatures human, part-human, and non-human associated with them; poems and stories about the early heroes of Denmark, Norway, and Sweden, and the shores of the Baltic generally; historical or, more frequently, quasi-historical tradition persistent in the corporate folk-memory, and highly regarded there; together with all such reinforcements of primitive grotesquerie as lay ready to the storyteller's hand. There is reminiscence in *Völsunga Saga* of the Burgundian catastrophe of the fifth century, and in *Hrólfs Saga Kraka* of dynastic struggles in fifth- and sixth-century Denmark and Sweden, but all of it so embedded in non-historical material that next to nothing historical can be deduced from them.

Thus, the opening chapters of the most celebrated of all Sagas of Olden Times, *Völsunga Saga*, those conducting to the birth of Sigmund (whom we have already met in *Beowulf* as dragon-killer, mound-despoiler, and uncle not father of Fitela), cannot manage without Sigi the son of Odinn, Odinn himself, a conquering expedition to Hunland, a valkyrie transformed into a crow, conception by eating an apple, a six-years pregnancy and a caesarean delivery ('As might be expected, the lad was a good size when he came to light. They say he kissed his mother ere she died'), the marriage of this lad Volsung (*volsi*, a phallus) to the valkyrie who had brought his father the apple, the resultant birth of Sigmund, and Volsung's noble hall in which 'stood a big tree, whose branches spread out through the roof, while its trunk extended down into the hall, and they called it Barnstokk, or child-trunk.' Between the birth of Sigmund and that of Sinfjotli there is no abatement of marvels: a visit from Odinn, who sank a sword up to its hilt in the Barnstokk apple-tree, saying that the man who succeeded in pulling it out should have it as his gift; Sigmund so succeeding, and thereby incurring the enmity of his brother-in-law-to-be, king Siggeir; the intrepid Volsung at the dictate of honour marching boldly into the trap laid for him, so that he fell with all his men, save for his ten sons who were captured alive; their being set in stocks in the forest, where in nine nights an old she-wolf devoured nine of them; the face and mouth of the survivor, Sigmund, being smeared with honey, so that when the she-wolf came to devour him in his turn she thrust her tongue into his mouth after the sweet bait and had it torn out by the dauntless man (the she-wolf, some men say, was king Siggeir's mother); and so by way of infanticide, shape-shifting, and incest between brother and sister, to the conception and birth of Sinfjotli, a true Volsung on both sides, and so hardy that when his mother sewed his tunic on to his arms, stitching through skin and flesh, he did not flinch. When she stripped the tunic from him, so that the skin came away with the sleeves, she warned that it would hurt him, but, 'No Volsung would think much of a hurt like that', he replied, and so was sent to his father for training. Through an act of inadvertency typical of the *Fornaldar Sögur* this included a period in wolf-shape.

This sequence of mainly savage wonders has not been recounted in order to belittle *Völsunga Saga*, whose author has substantial claims on our gratitude. The material is interesting in itself, and a necessary prelude to wonders to come: Sigurd, Reginn and Fafnir, the ring, the treasure, the shards of the sword Gram, and the dragon-killing; the wooings and marriages of Sigurd, Gunnar, Brynhild and Gudrun; the killing of Sigurd, Gudrun's marriage to Atli, and his destruction of her brothers Hogni and Gunnar, followed by her slaughter of her own sons and husband; her marriage to king Jonak, and the events leading to the deaths of Svanhild, king Jormunrekk, and the brothers Hamthir, Sorli, and Erp. The saga also preserves in not very distinguished prose the substance of the heroic poems, otherwise irrecoverable, which are presumed to have occupied the lost section, probably eight leaves, of the *Poetic Edda*.

Such finds as this Eddaic paraphrase in *Völsunga Saga*, the prose version of the lost poem *Bjarkamál* in *Hrólfs Saga*, and, most striking of all, the three poems preserved in *Hervarar Saga*—that relating to the battle of the Goths and the Huns, the so-called 'Waking of Angantyr', and the Riddles of Gestumblindi—remind us how earnestly the compilers of legendary sagas worked the deep veins of ancient tradition. This is why these sagas, apart from their often confined and normally censured interest as literary artefacts, are of

major importance for the analogues and illustrations they provide
for more august productions (our English *Beowulf* among them),
and the signposts, now beckoning, now cautionary, they set in the
wilderness of northern pre-history. The genre has even been
divided into categories of its own: sagas connected with the themes
of Eddaic poetry; those that present an all-too-strenuous viking
image; and those concerned almost entirely with the impossible
adventures of incredible heroes in improbable places (for which
Völsunga Saga, Hrólfs Saga Kraka, and *Bósa Saga ok Herrauðs* may be
proffered as examples). If we would have marvels, to seek is to find
—whether it be the archetypal irreconcilable, Starkad the Old, anti-
feminist flea-catcher and conscience of kings; Godmund the wizard-
king of Glaesivellir; Gunnar who died of snakes in the land of the
Huns, and Ragnar Hairybreeks who died of snakes in England;
Arrow-Odd who lasted two centuries, and Nornagest who endured
three. These and their like, Sigurd-Siegfried, Gudrun, Hrolf,
Harald Wartooth, Sigurd Hring, Egill One-hand, Bosi and Herraud,
Half and Half's champions, live at full stretch through their hybrid
chronicles. Never were deeds more daring and heroes more head-
strong, wonders more fluent or poured from less continent vials.
They carry heroic excess to inhuman heights and wondertale horrors
to subhuman depths, deal unspeakable wounds in unmentionable
places, and when the need arises offer an *ars amatoria* rank as a horse-
drench. Eagles, hawks, boars, bears, amazons, berserks, dragons,
sorceresses, shape-shifters, giants, hags, and assorted rudesters
abound; there are gods, dwarfs, trolls, talismans, tokens, tortures,
hints of ritual and evidences of cult. And, by no means least, human
relations are in the main immature, for the most part insensitive,
and as often as not insensate.

All of which sounds fine or deplorable according to taste. Either
way the legendary sagas as they are preserved in Icelandic manuscripts of a late date, or are to be discerned wholly or in part in
Saxo's *Danish History* much earlier, have entertained a great many
people of all ranks and classes over a very long period of time. The
Norwegian king Sverri thought these *lygisögur* or fictitious tales the
most entertaining of all, and with the saga of the she-troll Huld the
historian Sturla Thordarson won the goodwill of the Norwegian

queen of king Magnus. At the dawn of scientific criticism three hundred years ago the great Arni Magnusson took a poor view of them because they were heedless of truth, and they continue to be judged to their disadvantage today because they are not family histories. But such remote academic considerations disturbed their proper audience not at all. They gave their listener the ever-sought reverse of rationalization, sober heroism, humane standards, and pragmatically conducted narrative. They nourished him with foaming hornfuls drawn from the deep casks of wonder, myth, shamanism, make-believe, wish-fulfilment, unreason, for whose strong liquor few wholly lose a taste. Theirs is a supra-rational, surrealistic world in which anything goes—and mayhem, mirth and magic most of all. They please as the *Arabian Nights* please, and westerns and thrillers and science fiction, deeply and in one protean form or another permanently, and none the less because they are in large degree escapist art, blatantly motivated and arbitrarily portrayed. And sometimes by a wild inflation of the viking image, and sometimes by a wild parody of it, they gave the northern world the satisfaction of pride in the image and the equal satisfaction of laughing at it.

But our announced concern is with just one of these works of entertainment, *Hrólfs Saga Kraka*, and there more particularly with the most famous Bear's Son of northern literature, Bothvar Bjarki.[1] The saga in its written as in its oral form was a popular one. It exists in thirty-eight manuscripts, ranging with a relishable eccentricity from the second half of the seventeenth century to the opening years of the twentieth. These manuscripts derive from a common original written in the second half of the sixteenth century, but there is a fair consensus of opinion that the saga was put into

[1] The original name of our hero was Bjarki (Little Bear), the son of Björn (Bear) and Bera (She-Bear). He won his nickname *böðvar* (Warlike) for his prowess in battle. According to the poem styled *Bjarkamál*, the 'Lay of Bjarki', preserved in Saxo's translation in his *Danish History*, the precise occasion was his slaughter of Agnarus son of Ingellus with the sword Snyrtir, 'from which I won the nickname Warlike, *belligeri cognomen*'. This answers exactly to the Icelandic *böðvar*, gen. sing. of *böð*, O.E. *beadu*, battle. Böðvar-Bjarki is just such a name as Víga-Glúmr, 'Killer-Glum', and Hólmgöngu-Bersi, 'Wager-of-battle-Bersi'. In course of time the martial cognomen was in various sources, including *Hrólfs Saga*, taken to be the personal name and the personal name Bjarki to be the cognomen.

more or less its present shape near the year 1400. But a legendary saga about Hrolf and a heroic poem about Bjarki were used by Saxo Grammaticus for his *Danish History c.* 1200; the unknown author of the lost *Skjöldunga Saga,* also *c.* 1200, of which we possess a summary in Latin prepared by the Icelandic humanist Arngrímur Jónsson in the last years of the sixteenth century for his *Regum Danicarum Fragmenta* (1596), was well-versed in Hrolfian tradition, and probably made more extensive reference to Bjarki than the two brief mentions preserved by Arngrímur. In any case, that Hrolf was important in Danish genealogies and legends, and Bjarki (Bothvar Bjarki, Bodvarus) known early as his champion and son-in-law is amply attested. Nor need we doubt that Hrolf's saga was one to attract fictitious accretions as it descended through the centuries. An intriguing item of information in these earliest records is the statement in *Bjarkarímur,* of *c.* 1400 (in all probability filtered through *Skjöldunga Saga*), that Bothvar Bjarki and Hjalti were prominent among the champions sent by king Hrolf to help king Athils of Uppsala in the 'battle on the ice of Lake Väner', which that warlike Swede planned against his rival king Ali of the Upplands (*Bjarkarímur,* VIII, stanzas 17–18, 22–8). This is a close parallel to the passage in *Beowulf* (2391–6) which tells how Beowulf befriended the hapless Eadgils and lent him his support 'across the wide water' (*ofer sæ síde*); and so vigorously righted his wrongs in 'cold and grievous raids (campaigns)' (*cealdum cear-síðum*) that their common enemy lost his life. There is little critical dissent from the equations Eadgils-Athils and Onela-Ali; and that Bear (Beowulf) and Little Bear (Bjarki) are cast for the same role in the clash between these two monarchs can hardly be accident or coincidence. Beowulf and Bjarki have other things in common, but for the moment it is sufficient to notice that this tradition of Bjarki's intervention in the affairs of the Uppsala king is an old one, and in oral form must considerably antedate *Skjöldunga Saga;* though there are reasons for thinking that *Hrólfs Saga* in the form in which we now have it is later than 1200 (perhaps by two hundred years) and maybe substantially influenced by *Skjöldunga Saga.*[1]

[1] See Jakob Benediktsson, 'Icelandic Traditions of the Scyldings', *Saga-Book,* XV (1957–9), pp. 48–66, and esp. 54–7 and 65–6.

In style and content the saga is a romantic retelling of the legendary history of three generations of the Skjoldung kings of Denmark: first, the brothers Frothi and Halfdan; second, the sons of Halfdan, Hroar and Helgi; and third, the son of Helgi, that Hrolf who was known as Hrolf Kraki. Here is a first summary of it:

There were two brothers in Denmark, Frothi and Halfdan by name, king's sons, and each of them ruling his own kingdom. 'King Halfdan was genial and gentle, gracious and good-natured, but king Frothi was a downright savage.' Impelled by envy and a natural brutishness Frothi burned king Halfdan's house over his head, then had him killed. Halfdan's sons Helgi and Hroar were saved from destruction by their foster-father Reginn, and safeguarded on an island by the wizard-shepherd Vifil. Later they found lodging in the house of Jarl Saevil, who had married their sister Signy. They were unruly lads of doltish mien. With the help of their sister and foster-father they took vengeance on their wicked uncle by burning him to death in his royal hall. Helgi, the older and more assertive brother, ruled over Denmark, and Hroar married the king of Northumberland's daughter and shared his royal power.

For a long while Helgi remained unwed, and when at last he took a wife (and no lesser word than 'take' does justice to Helgi's courtships) his bride was none other than his own daughter Yrsa, herself the product of a rape upon the body of the warrior-queen Olof of Germany, a lady of such amazonian deeds and physique, and so versed in the noble art of self-defence, that one marvels less that Helgi failed in his first attempt than that he succeeded at his second. The fruit of this unknowingly incestuous union of father and daughter was Hrolf, and when Helgi was ambushed and killed by Yrsa's second husband, king Athils of the Uppsala Swedes, Hrolf succeeded to the kingdom. (If we ask ourselves what kingdom, in sixth-century Denmark, we can but echo the rhetorical plaint of Saxo Grammaticus in the Preface to his *Danish History: Quis enim res Danie gestas literis prosequeretur?* 'Who *could* write a record of the deeds of Denmark?')

One of king Helgi's treasures had been a ring so famed, and also so precious, that he gave it to his brother Hroar for half the Danish kingdom. This cost Hroar his life, at the hands of his nephew Hrok.

The ring was thrown into the sea, but when Hroar's son Agnarr was twelve years old he dived in and brought it up.

When next we hear of Hrolf he is being extolled as the mightiest, most generous, most warlike and victorious of all kings, with a courtful of champions at Lejre. He had two daughters, and a half-sister named Skuld, begotten by his father on a laithsome ladye of folktale and destined to be his baneswoman. To his court come the greatest warriors of the Northlands, including Bothvar Bjarki. In course of time he determines to seek his patrimony from king Athils at Uppsala and survives various well-mounted exercises in grammarye by Athils and the god Odinn before getting safely home again. But Odinn was now his foe and the tide of his destruction rolling forward. His half-sister Skuld (her name means Debt or Due) had been given in marriage to king Hjorvarth, whom Hrolf tricked into becoming his tributary, thereby lacerating her wifely pride. By a counter-trick husband and wife brought a countless multitude of armed men, backed by witchcraft, sorcery, elves, and norns, to Lejre, where Hrolf and his champions were holding their Yuletide feast. In a night assault, during which a huge bear toiled for the defence, and a huge boar for the attackers, king Hrolf and all his champions perished of sword and fire, together with king Hjorvarth and most of his army. A cruel vengeance was exacted on queen Skuld.

The first thing to say about this ragout of Skjoldung history is that it is not always at one with itself and frequently at sixes and sevens with its analogues. According to Sven Aageson's twelfth-century version of these matters, it was Halfdan (Haldan) who killed Frothi, and this is repeated in the fourteenth-century *Series Runica Regum Daniae Altera*. Also, while all sources agree that Halfdan was a mighty king, they cannot agree whether he was mighty good or mighty bad. In Saxo's account he was the son not the brother of Frothi; his brothers were Roe (Hroar) and Scatus, his equals in valour and princely ambition. He slew them both and maltreated their adherents after the fashion of Frothi in *Hrólfs Saga*. 'The most notable thing in the fortunes of Haldanus', comments Saxo, 'was this, that though he devoted every instant of his life to cruel deeds, yet he died of old age, and not by the steel.' His two songs were named Ro and Helgo. *Skjöldunga Saga* has him killed by his half-brother Ingialldus; *Bjarkarímur* by a full brother of that name; and other sources present other confusions. In the face of such contradictory witness it is prudent if insular to conclude only that there was a Skjoldung Halfdan, that he was the same person, or figure, as the 'high Healfdene' of *Beowulf*, and therefore the father of Hroar and Helgi (Hrothgar and Halga).

As for Hroar, no weight should be allowed to the late thirteenth-century *Annales Ryenses*, which makes him Helgi's father; none to the *Chronicle of Lejre* (*Chronicon Lethrense*), c. 1170, which makes him the son of king Dan of Denmark and his wife Dania (than which nothing could be more Danic), and the father of Helgi and Halfdan; and none to the *Series Runica*, which makes him the son of Frothi. Both the Old English *Widsith* (which antedates these other written sources by at least four centuries) and the Icelandic *Skjöldunga Saga* record that Hroar, in company with either his nephew Hrolf or his brother Helgi, took violent and successful action against Ingeld-Ingialldus, who in that saga is named as the brother and killer of their father Halfdanus. The *Widsith* entry is one of the best-known in the *Beowulf-Hrólfs Saga* context: 'For a long, long time that nephew and uncle, Hrothulf and Hrothgar, kept the peace together, after they had driven away the viking race, made Ingeld's vanguard stoop, cut down at Heorot the Heathobardan host' (45-9). Saxo's account of Ro is short and spare as the stature he ascribes to him: he founded the town known as Roskildia, and was thrice attacked and eventually killed by a Swedish king Hothbroddus. The *Chronicle of Lejre* agrees that he built Roskilde by the Isafjord, and named it partly after himself and partly after the very beautiful spring (*kilde*) he found there, though our soberer modern conjecture connects the spring with horses not with Ro. The *Chronicle* adds that king Ro lived in such peace and tranquillity that none drew sword against him, nor did he himself lead an expedition abroad. *Hrólfs Saga* on the other hand has him spend long years with king Northri of Northumberland as his land's stay and defender, till he married Ogn the king's daughter, and in time succeeded to the kingdom and ruled it till he was killed by the infamous Hrok, who coveted his famous ring, elsewhere called Svíagriss. Into the tangle of names and relationships represented by the Old English Hrethric (in *Beowulf* and in *Beowulf* alone said to be Hrothgar's, i.e. Hroar's, son), the Norse Hraerekr and Hrokkr, and the Latin Raerecus, Roricus, and Rokil(?), there is no need to enter, except to remark that a determined sorting of one of Saxo's more obvious muddles leads to the conclusion that Hrolf killed a Roricus who seems to have been a king of the Danes, just as a reading of *Beowulf* leads to the conclusion that Hrothulf killed a Hrethric who was the son of Hrothgar, king of the Danes. True, *Hrólfs Saga* describes Hroar as a king of Northumberland in England, and *Skjöldunga Saga* says that Roas (Hroar) married the daughter of an English king, but to find significance in such fortuitous reference for the presence of a Danish king Hrothgar in the English poem *Beowulf* is surely perilous and probably absurd.

Of that other distinguished Skjoldung, Hrolf Kraki, we have said enough in our summary of his saga to indicate that he was a worthy scion of his illustrious and puzzling forebears. It is in a context of these violent, picturesque, and highly romanticized figures, and their violent, picturesque, and highly romanticized biographies, that we now encounter the compound of wondertale, hero-tale, and legendary history which in various of the manuscripts of *Hrólfs Saga* is ushered in by some such title as *Böðvars þáttr og Bræðra hans*. This 'Story of Bothvar and his Brothers' terminates formally when Hott-Hjalti is given the sword Gullinhjalti, but the saga continues to treat of Bothvar as Hrolf's champion till his death at Lejre. Here is a minimal summary of Bothvar's story as it appears in *Hrólfs Saga*:

In Uppdalir in Norway three sons were born at a birth to a commoner's daughter. Their father was a king's son who was a bear by day and a man by night. They had the traditional unruly youth of the Bear's Son, and each found it necessary to leave home. The son came to the court of king Hrolf at Lejre, where he distinguished himself by his ferocity and strength, became a king's champion, and carried out various perilous tasks. He took part in Hrolf's last stand against his foes at Lejre, for some of the time in bear-form, and died with his lord.[1]

[1] For an analysis of the Bear's Son prototypes see A–T 301, 'The Three Stolen Princesses', I and Motifs I, quoted on pp. 8–9 above, and A–T 650A, 'Strong

15. SPEARSMEN WITH BOAR-CRESTED HELMETS
From Torslunda

These unadorned sentences indicate that Bothvar Bjarki has a twofold role in story. He is both Bear's Son and King's Champion. Some accounts of him concentrate on the one, some on the other. *Hrólfs Saga* finds room for both. To begin with, it offers us an unambiguous, if complicated, account of a bear's son's parentage, begetting, youth, adventures, and death; and the medieval Icelandic ballad cycle concerning Bjarki, the *Bjarkarímur*, while adding to the complications, reinforces the thesis. But in the *Danish History* of Saxo Grammaticus (i.e. the Lettered) we find a Biarco, and in *Skjöldunga Saga* a Bodvarus, described by both as the foremost champion of the foremost king of the North, the Danish king Hrolf, but without smack or smell of beardom. When further we note that the Biarco of the *Bjarkamál*, that famous, ancient, and heroic poem preserved for posterity in the self-satisfied hexameters of Saxo, is nopart bear but all-part human, it grows clear that Bjarki (as we shall

---

John', the more relevant portions of which are:
I. *The Strong Youth.* (*a*) *The strong youth is the son of a bear or* (b) a woman of the sea or the woods, or (c) he is born from an egg, or (d) is struck from iron by a smith, or (e) he is the son of a man (dream) and a troll-woman. (f) He sucks his mother for many years. (g) He practices his strength by uprooting trees.
II. *His Setting-forth.* (a) On account of his enormous appetite *he is sent from home.* (b) He works for a smith but drives the anvil into the ground and (c) throws trees on to the roof and breaks it. (d) He has a giant cane made which holds fifty cattle, or (e) he sets forth on adventures.
    The relevant motifs are:
    I. B631. *Human offspring from marriage to animal. F611.1.1. Strong man son of bear who has stolen his mother.* F611.1.14. Strong hero son of woman of sea. F611.1.15. Strong hero son of woodspirit. F611.1.11. Strong hero born from egg. F611.1.12. Strong hero struck by smith from iron. F611.1.13. Strong hero son of man and troll-woman. Relations take place in dream. T516. Conception through dream. *F611.2.3. Strong hero's long nursing.* F611.2.1. Strong hero suckled by animal. F611.3.1. Strong hero practices uprooting trees.
    II. L114.3. *Unruly hero.* F612.1. Strong hero sent from home because of enormous appetite. *F612.2. Strong hero kills (overcomes) playmates; sent from home.* F614.1. Strong man drives anvil into ground. F614.6. Strong man throws trees on roof and breaks it. F614.2. Strong man uproots tree and uses it as a weapon. F612.3.1. Giant cane for strong man. Cane holds fifty cattle. *H.1221. Quest for adventure.*
    Sections III and IV deal with the strong man's *Labor Contract* and *Labors.* The second part of Bothvar Bjarki's story is reinforced by extraordinary companions: see A–T 513, 'The Helpers' II and III, quoted on pp. 69–70 above.

16. WEAPONS AND ARMOUR FROM THE VENDEL GRAVES

henceforth commonly call him) is a hero of the same general type as Beowulf. He is attached, that is, to two worlds of story, that of the international wondertale, and that of Germanic, or more specifically Scandinavian, heroic tradition associated with the Danish royal line of the Skjoldungs. Beowulf's association is with Hroar-Hrothgar, Bjarki's with that monarch's nephew Hrólfr-Hrothulf.

First, then, the folktale hero, the Bear's Son, as his origins and the first half of his life are recorded in the fourth section of *Hrólfs Saga*, 'The Story of Bothvar and his Brothers':

There was a prince north in Norway by the name of Bjorn (*Björn*, Bear). He was the son of king Hring who when Bjorn's mother died sent men forth to find him a second wife. They found her in a house in Finnmark, the daughter of a Lapp king, her name Hvit or White. She was young and found king Hring rather old. Bjorn had a sweet-heart, a commoner's daughter named Bera (She-Bear). When Hring was away at the wars this wicked stepmother Hvit suggested that she and Bjorn her son-in-law share the same bed, but he rewarded her invitation with a box on the ear. In turn she struck him with her wolf-skin gloves, declaring he should become a cave-bear, fierce and savage, and never win free of this dire enchantment. Whereupon Bjorn vanished away, and a monstrous grey bear began to prey on the king's flock and herds. One evening Bera encountered the bear and followed it to its cave, where she found Bjorn Hringsson in human form again. She lived with him by night, when he was a man, but not by day. Soon king Hring returned home and somewhat against his will was persuaded by queen Hvit to hunt down the bear which was ravaging his stock. Bjorn, in bear form, died like a bear, in a ring of men and dogs.

During their last night together Bjorn told Bera how she would bear him three sons, and that she must on no account eat of his bear's flesh. However, the wicked Hvit forced her to swallow one mouthful and one grain. She had a bad pregnancy, and in time was delivered of three sons. Elgfrothi was an elk from the navel down; Thorir Houndsfoot had hound's feet on him from the instep; Bothvar Bjarki (Little Bear) the last born was without blemish. All three were fierce and unsparing young men. Their father had left them a weapon apiece: a sax or short-sword for Elgfrothi, an axe for

Thorir, and a wondrous sword for Bothvar. These they took one by one and departed, but before Bothvar left he whipped a shrunken skin bag over the head of the sorceress Hvit, tied it under her chin, and publicly beat her to death. When his grandfather king Hring died he succeeded to the kingdom, but knew no happiness in it. On his travels he met and wrestled with his brother Elgfrothi, who gave him blood to drink from his elk-leg.

Afterwards Frothi stamped with his foot on the rock which stood beside him right up to the pastern. 'I will come to this hoof-mark every day, and find what is in the print. It will be earth if you are dead of sickness; water, if you are dead of drowning; blood, if you are dead of weapons—and then I will avenge you, for I love you best of all mankind.' (p. 276)

He next proceeded to Gautland, where his brother Thorir had been made king. He was mistaken for Thorir, and lay chastely abed, outside the coverlets, with his brother's wife until Thorir's return.

Thereafter his travels took him from Gautland to Denmark, where he arrived at a humble dwelling and got a direction for king Hrolf's court at Lejre. He arrived there in a high-handed way and found the craven Hott hiding behind a shieldwall of bones from the brutality of the retainers. He protected him, killed one of his assailants, and took service with king Hrolf. Towards Yule the retainers grew downcast, because for the last two years the royal precincts had been invaded by a huge and horrible winged monster, on which weapons would not bite, and which killed the bravest of the Danes who opposed it. Hrolf ordered his men to stay clear of it and leave the cattle to their fate. Bothvar disobeyed the king, dragged Hott along with him, killed the creature with his wondrous but for a time unwilling blade, and made Hott drink of its blood and eat of its heart, at which he grew strong and brave. By a trick he later makes it appear as though Hott killed the creature, whereupon the king gave Hott a new name Hjalti (Hilt-guard or pommel) after the sword he had used, Gullinhjalti (Goldenhilt). He was also styled Hjalti the Magnanimous.

Later in the winter the king's twelve berserks returned home from the wars and offered their customary man-matching challenge to the liegemen in hall. Bothvar promptly knocked their leader senseless and was promoted to the seat at the king's right hand. 'The king', we are instructed,

allowed these men of his to practise sports and crafts of every kind, together with all sorts of games and entertainments. Bothvar proved himself the foremost of all his champions, whatever need be taken in hand, and he came into such great honour with king Hrolf that he married Drifa, his only daughter[1] (pp. 287–8).

If we were to seek the precise moment in Bothvar Bjarki's story when he moves from a purely wondertale to a mainly heroic milieu, this of his marriage to Drifa and consequent kinship with king Hrolf is probably it.[2] One could fairly argue that his dealings with Hott, the winged monster, and the berserks are marked by a crude buffoonery which keeps them in line with various feats and stratagems attributed to the Strong John of folktale, and that it is only when he is seen mixing with kings and champions and taking part in events enshrined in historical tradition that his transition to a different level of story becomes effective. Even so, folktale motifs continue to be attached to him, his adventures remain heavy with magic and enchantment, and when his life moves to its climax we are again presented with his bear-image as his fetch or animal-spirit strikes men down with his forepaws or crunches them in his heavy jaws.

Not that all or even a preponderance of the folktale motifs of *Hrólfs Saga* are peculiar to the Bear's Son. They establish themselves early, and long before Bothvar Bjarki appears on the scene. In the first part of the saga, 'The Story of Frothi', Halfdan's two sons, Hroar and Helgi, are let owe their lives to a trick in which they are called by the names of a shepherd's dogs; later when they visit their wicked uncle they put just such an antic madness on as the young Amlethus-Hamlet, including the remarkable detail of Helgi (under

---

[1] By Saxo's account Bjarki married Hrolf's sister, Ruta; by *Skjöldunga Saga*'s, Hrolf's daughter, Scura, who is named once only in *Hrólfs Saga*.
[2] His exploits as king Hrolf's champion are set out later, in the appropriate areas of chapters 2 and 3.

the pseudonym Ham) riding a colt face-to-tail. They have a faithful fosterfather who in dumb show counsels them how to destroy the usurper, and there is a riddling variation on the Polyphemus-theme when Frothi finds himself trapped in his hall by the boys and their helpers, including their fosterfather Reginn, but his men cannot understand his anxiety because rain is outside (*Reginn*, the personal name, and *regn*, rain, have practically the same sound).

In the second section of the saga, that concerning the sons of Halfdan, Helgi Halfdansson's eccentric style of wooing is sufficient in itself to involve him in folktale difficulties. So crude an amorist should have beaten out his nuptials on an anvil with a hammer, and let poor females lie alone. On the evening of his forced bridal with the amazonian Olof he gets helplessly drunk, is pricked with a sleepthorn, shorn and shaved of all his hair, tarred, and dumped back at his ships. He gets his revenge by faring like a beggar into her kingdom and inveigling her into the forest under pretence of a gift of treasure. The fruit of this dear revenge was the girl-child Yrsa, unloved by her reluctant mother, named after her mother's dog, and at twelve years of age set to tend the royal sheep. As befitted her folktale status she won her prince—even better, her king—but, alas, no other king than the indefatigable Helgi, revisiting those shores and 'curious to know what had happened there'. Yrsa says she is a peasant's daughter. 'You have not thrall's eyes', says he, and carries her off to his ships and kingdom, and marries her. Their son was Hrolf, after whom the saga is named. When in course of time the still revengeful Olof revealed that Helgi had married his own daughter, Yrsa left him, and Helgi slept in a house apart, with no companions, awaiting his next wondertale vicissitude.

Then one Yule-even, when king Helgi had gone to bed and there was foul weather abroad, the story goes that there came a knocking, a rather faint knocking, at the door. It struck him how unkingly it would be to leave this benighted creature outside when he might help it, so he went and opened the door, and saw how some poor tattered creature had come there. It spoke—'This is well done of you, king'— and then came inside the house.

'Cover yourself with straw and a bearskin,' said the king, 'that you may not freeze to death.'

'Share your bed with me, sire,' it pleaded. 'I would sleep alongside you, for my very life is at stake.'

'My gorge rises at you,' said the king, 'but if it is as you say, then lie here in your clothes at the bed's edge, and then it will not harm me.'

She did so, and the king turned the other way from her. There was a light burning in the house, and after a while he peered over his shoulder at her, and saw that it was a woman lying there, so lovely that he thought he had never before beheld woman more fair. She was dressed in a gown of silk. He turned to her quickly and joyfully, but, 'I wish to take my leave now,' she told him. 'You have released me from hard durance, for this was my stepmother's curse on me, and many kings have I visited in their homes. Do not now end with wickedness. It is not my wish to stay here any longer.'

'No, no,' said the king, 'there can be no question of your leaving so soon. We will not part so. And now we must patch up a wedding for you, for you please me greatly.'

'It is for you to command, sire,' she said, and they slept together that night. Then in the morning she had this to say: 'Now that you have subjected me to your lust, you may know this, that we will have a child. Now, king, do as I tell you. Come to collect our child at this same time next winter at your boathouse. If you do not, you shall pay for it.' And with that she went away.

King Helgi was now in somewhat better spirits than before. Time wore on, but to this he paid no heed. Then after a three years' interval it happened that three men came riding to this same house where the king lay sleeping. It was midnight. They had with them a girl child and set her down near the house. The woman who had brought the child had this to say: 'Know, king,' she said, 'that your kinsfolk must pay for this, that you set at naught the thing I bade you. Yet you yourself shall reap the benefit that you freed me from the spell laid upon me. Know too that this girl's name is Skuld. She is our daughter.' (pp. 246–8)

The third section of *Hrólfs Saga*, 'The Story of Svipdag' is about a youngest son who leaves home, achieves success by acts of valour, and becomes the foremost warrior of the disreputable but famous Athils, king of the Swedes. Disgusted with Athils's personal treachery, he leaves him for the court of king Hrolf, taking his two brothers with him. There are strong resemblances to parts of 'The

Story of Bothvar', which straightway follows. Like Bothvar, Svip-dag is a third and youngest son; he is very strong; he tests the power and malignancy of king Athils; he takes service with king Hrolf, and at Hrolf's court has a similar sort of adventure with the king's man-matching berserks. Like Bothvar he starts as a figure of wondertale and comes to enjoy a more legendary ambience.

'The Story of Bothvar and his Brothers' as defined formally by the saga-writer or his scribe, from its opening with Hring and Bjorn in Uppdalir, Norway, to Bothvar's marriage to king Hrolf's daughter, is all folktale. The Bear's Son, the cruel (and amorous) stepmother, the sword in the stone, the chaste brother, the killing of the monster—these are its chief ingredients, and they have already been outlined. The story of the Bear's Son told in verse form in *Bjarkarímur* (*c.* 1400) is even more involved with bears and bear-dom. Here there are two Bothvars, father and son, the first like Bjorn hunted down and killed in bear form, the second born with a bear's claw on his toe. Like our Bjarki he kills the wicked Hvit and arrives in the neighbourhood of Hrolf's court at Lejre. What follows is strongly reminiscent of that part of the Welsh story of *Culhwch and Olwen* which tells us of Culhwch's arrival at the mound and home of Custennin the shepherd. He found a peasant and his wife, from whom he heard about the perils of Hrolf's court: a big stone which twelve men could hardly lift; two savage watchdogs at the gates; fierce sports and bone-throwing within. Like Custennin and his wife the couple have a son, at present under a cloud, but destined to play a hero's part later in the saga. The old woman gives him two loaves of bread with which to distract the dogs' jaws from his person; and just as Culhwch and his helpers won their way into Ysbaddaden's fort by killing nine gateman and nine mastifs (p. 76), and Cúchulainn made entry into the house of Culann by kill-ing a hound so fierce and strong that it took three chains and three men on each chain to hold him, so Bjarki forced an entry into Hrolf's hall by killing two gallows-tikes and two champions. Where Ysbaddaden threw spears, Hrolf's men threw bones, and in each case the missile was thrown back with painful consequence. Among the achievements that followed it was not a winged monster that Bjarki slew, and Hjalti was thought to have slain, but a she-wolf and a grey bear, and it was by virtue of three draughts of the she-wolf's blood that Hjalti grew brave and strong as a troll. Saxo has nothing to tell of winged monster or she-wolf, but is content to let Bjarki kill a bear.

For he met a huge bear in a thicket, and slew it with a javelin; and then bade his companion Hjalti put his lips to the beast and drink the blood that came out, that he might be the stronger afterwards. For it was believed that a draught of this sort caused an increase of bodily strength (II, 56).

And Saxo is right. That the strength, valour, wisdom, sexuality or other nature of a slain man or beast can be acquired by partaking of him is among the most persistent and widespread beliefs of hopeful, baffled man, and a prominent feature of his religions, medicaments, and story-telling.

Finally the *Bjarkarímur* add a detail to the Bear's Son's story unrecorded by *Hrólfs Saga* or Saxo. It concerns the defeat and killing of Agnarr, a hero who dealt out not wounds or scratches, but swept off five heads at a blow, or with one sweep of his mighty sword split three men asunder each side of him.

The bold Hrólfr cried aloud: 'Where are you, valiant Bjarki? Show us your great might, you who love battle!'
Fearlessly Bothvarr drew and flourished Laufi, and then men fled from him like children. The fighters saw a white bear running among them; Agnarr himself laid his hard sword on this bear's head, but it broke at the hilts, to his great grief. Then Laufi ripped his life out, as Bjarki took part in the game; he drove the naked blade in the chieftain's breast, and it reached its mark on him. The bright blade pierced the heart of the mighty heir of a prince; all men saw how Agnarr laughed—such men are a great loss. The berserk died smiling, breathing out hot breath; they all thought Agnarr had been overcome by a cunning trick (VIII, 6–12).

The colour of this *hvítbjörn* or white bear invites speculation. We should normally expect a *grábjörn*, literally a grey but in fact almost any un-white bear. Is it an Icelandic, or even a Greenlandic, contribution to the Bear's Son's much convoluted story? Iceland, like Denmark, had no white bears of its own, but unlike Denmark occasionally acquired one, usually in the north and northwest of the country, ferried over by ice-floe from Greenland. The only white bear to be seen in Denmark would be one brought overseas, as we know they sometimes were, as a gift to a very great lord. But whatever the origin of this exotic new contribution to the Bear's Son's story, it is welcome. Of all bears the polar bear is the most awesome, mysterious and majestic, even at the beginning of his life's course of peril and rapine—like Knud Rasmussen's Bear in the Ice-hole, 'a young male, a regal wanderer of the wastes, resplendent in a long-haired yellowish coat which sparkled in its fresh-grown glory, a combat-trained full-size giant come from the open sea.' How should the Bear's Son's stature not be enhanced and his image magnified by so rare and splendid a transmogrification?

2. King's Champion

We said earlier, when discussing the substance or story-content of *Beowulf*, that a proportion of the heroic legend in that poem was itself emergent from wondertale. This is true of *King Hrolf's Saga* also. A summary of the second part of Bothvar Bjarki's story, by now in large measure subjected to Hrolf's, will show how wondertale motif, folk belief, and superstition continue to be prominent even in the more 'heroic' period of his life. Hrolf's champions, and in this they remind us strongly of the role and nature of Arthur's warriors in *Culhwch and Olwen*, are also his helping companions on a quest for treasure in a warlock-monarch's hall, with a more than mortal resistance to thirst, cold, and heat. The wooden pillar in king Athils's hall, into whose hollow he escapes at a supreme moment of peril, is not too unlike the Barnstokk tree in the hall of king Volsung, set there for protection and luck. The distraction of pursuers by treasures strewn in their path, golden apples, rings, combs and the like, is a widespread motif of story, as is the shearing off of an ignoble foe's buttocks (in this case king Athils's). The mutilation of Hrolf's Danish horses by a trouble-maker among the Swedes is similar to the mutilation of Matholwch's Irish horses by a trouble-maker among the Welsh—Efnisien in the Second Branch of the Mabinogi, 'Branwen daughter of Llŷr'.[1] We meet the animated

[1] 'This was promptly reported to king Athils, how closely they had laid down the law about the care of the horses. "This is the height of insolence and pride," said he. "Now, take my orders and do as I bid. Hack off their tail-bones as high as their spines, aye, flush with their rumps, and cut off their forelocks so that the skin of the forehead comes away with it, and in every way treat them as shamefully as you know how, except that you leave them still just alive, just alive."' *Hrólfs Saga* 27.

dead (as in 'Branwen', *Grettis Saga*, and so widely elsewhere) and the animal familiar, the hiding of hostile warriors about a hall and an adventure with fire (these two again as in 'Branwen'), and a faithful hound which comes to its master's rescue.[1] The heroic conventions are likewise prominent, service and reward, loyalty to one's lord, the practice of valour and pursuit of fame, and before the saga's end these have practically ousted the shifts, adjustments, reconciliations and self-preservations characteristic of the popular tale. The hero, whether king Hrolf or Bothvar Bjarki, has no choice between death or glory. They await him together, and he embraces them both. On the heroic level of story, Champions are more than Strong Helpers and must pay the price of their advancement. Thus:

During a costly banquet at Lejre king Hrolf asks one of those fatal questions that forbid peace or long life for heroes. Having looked to his right hand and his left, Did Bothvar, he asked, know of any king his equal or ruling over such champions? Bothvar confessed he did not, but added that he felt it a diminution of the royal dignity that Hrolf had never gone to recover those treasures of his father Helgi's which his father-in-law king Athils held on to so unjustly. Soon afterwards Hrolf set off for king Athils's court at Uppsala in Sweden with a hundred men, his twelve champions, and

---

'And thereupon, lo, one day, Efnisien the quarrelsome man we spoke of above happening upon the billets of Matholwch's horses, and he asked whose horses they were. "These are Matholwch's horses, king of Ireland," said they. "What are they doing there?" he asked. "The king of Ireland is here and has slept with Branwen thy sister; and these are his horses." "And is it thus they have done with a maiden so excellent as she, and my sister at that, bestowing her without my consent! They could have put no greater insult upon me", said he. And thereupon he set upon the horses and cut off their lips to the teeth, and their ears to their heads, and their tails to their backs, and wherever he could clutch their eyelids he cut them to the very bone. And he maimed the horses thus till there was no use could be made of the horses.' *Mabinogion*, p. 27.

[1] Olrik is sufficiently impressed by resemblances between Hrolf's expedition to Uppsala and Bendigeidfran's expedition to Ireland to see one (probably the Welsh story) as an influence, by way of England, upon the other (*Heroic Legends*, pp. 360 and 490). But visits to or raids upon grotesque and terrible halls in other kingdoms are common enough to require no theory of influences and transfers. In any case no wise scholastic elephant will put much weight on that weak English bridge.

his twelve berserks too. They arrived one nightfall at a farm and received hospitality at the farmer's hand. During the night it grew unbearably cold and many of Hrolf's men hunted around for extra covering. In the morning farmer Hrani advised king Hrolf that those of his men who could not stand a touch of cold would not be much use to him at Uppsala, and Hrolf sent half his force back home. The next night they came to another and smaller farm and seemed to recognize their host of the night before. This time the ordeal was by thirst, and the following night by heat and fire, and when king Hrolf rode onwards to Uppsala of all his host he kept but twelve—his champions—who though frozen, parched, and toasted as the rest of them, bore their ills unflinchingly. Their entrance into Uppsala was handsome and brisk, but to the Swedes offensive, and king Athils secretly gave orders that their stabled horses should be maltreated. King Hrolf and his champions, armoured and weaponed, and with hawks on their shoulders, advanced to the royal hall.

Its murk and menace within are a perfect setting for the treachery, ingratitude, savagery, and general craziness of the proceedings there. The Danes are put to the test of fire, which Hrolf survives with the aid of his fire-tested helping companions. Hrolf receives his curious nickname *kraki*, pole-ladder, because of his slight and unimpressive stature, and along with it a prophetic promise of revenge by his unlikely name-fastener. The champions are attacked by a rampaging supernatural boar, and defended by the helping hound Gram who rips the boar's ears off and his chops with them, in a manner reminiscent of many human folktale beard-flayings and shavings. Hrolf's hawk fights with and kills the hawks of king Athils, the champions cut their way out of their blazing lodging, and later ride off with Athils's treasure; and in a 'magic flight' across the Fyris plain Hrolf disrupts the Swedish pursuit by sowing the path with gold, so that the Swedes fling themselves from their horses and go scrabbling for gain. Athils himself stooped low over his horse to recover the wondrous ring Sviagríss, Pig of the Swedes, with his spearpoint, and as he so offered himself to the stroke Hrolf sheared off both his buttocks with the sword Skofnung. Towards nightfall the Danes reached a farm and went to the door, and who should be there but their old acquaintance, farmer Hrani. As before he offered them hospitality, and a gift of weapons too, but these last Hrolf would not accept. Hrani grew deeply offended, and they parted on bad terms. Too late they realized the identity of their host. Said Bothvar: 'I fear we acted not very wisely when we refused what we should have accepted—and maybe what we have refused is victory.' 'It must have been old Odinn', agreed king Hrolf. 'Quite certainly he was a man with one eye.' They reached home with their fame and foreboding.

Thereafter for a long while Hrolf and his champions sought no foreign wars and lived peacefully in Denmark. 'No one attacked them, all his tributary kings did him homage and paid him their tribute.' This is very reminiscent of Beowulf the Geat, who could say as his life drew to its close: 'I have ruled over this people fifty winters. There was no folk-king among my neighbours durst assault me in arms, oppress me with fear. I awaited my destiny in my own country, looked well to what was my own, picked no treacherous quarrels, swore few oaths unjustly.' But there is always an enemy: for Beowulf a dragon, for Hrolf a sorceress (and possibly, and even then possibly in error, a savage hart). In each case the blow fell from a clear sky, bringing Beowulf grief and foreboding, but leaving Hrolf at first indifferent and then exultant. Beowulf was troubled lest he had offended Almighty God; Hrolf must now pay the Skjoldung debt to the elvish world incurred by his father Helgi when he begat Skuld on an elf-woman and was heedless of the mother's wish. So now when Skuld and Hjorvarth came with their hidden host to Lejre, 'King Hrolf paid no heed to this. He was more concerned now with his munificence and pomp and pride and all that noble valour which filled his breast, with feasting all those who were come there, and that his glory be carried to the ends of the earth.' Even when he heard that the enemy was at the door there was no distress in him.

Then king Hrolf sprang up, and undaunted he spake. 'Let us take of that drink which is best, and we will drink before battle and be merry, and show in that fashion what men they are, Hrolf's champions, and strive for this alone, that our valour be never forgotten; for here are come the greatest and bravest champions of all neighbouring lands. Tell it to Hjorvarth, to Skuld, and those their bravoes, that we will drink to make us merry before we collect our tribute.' (p. 311)

In *Bjarkamál* the heroic note is still sharper, but save for one significant shift of emphasis the story it has to tell is much the same. The author of *Hrólfs Saga* is as committed to the supernatural in his account of Bothvar Bjarki's death as of his birth and begetting, but in Saxo's *Danish History*, where the *Bjarkamál* is preserved, Bjarki is not a bear's son, and Skuld no sorceress. Odinn is present at the death-struggle, and Bjarki sees and threatens him from under a valkyrie's arm, but there is no word of Odinn-Hrani and his ill-will to Hrolf. Save for Saxo's perfunctory reference to Elysium and Phlegethon, there is not even word of that other world where the valiant dead live with the War-God and wait for Ragnarok. The slain perish without enchantment's aid, and aidless lie slain for ever.

Not so in *Hrólfs Saga*. When Hrolf and his champions sprang up from their seats, left the good drink and begin their last fight, there was no sign of Bothvar Bjarki, whom they judged either captured or slain. What was seen by Hjorvarth and the assailants was

how a huge bear advanced before king Hrolf's men, and always next at hand where the king was. He killed more men with paw of his than any five of the king's champions. Blows and missiles rebounded from him, and he beat down both men and horses from king Hjorvarth's host, and everything within reach he crunched with his teeth, so that alarm and dismay arose in king Hjorvarth's host (p. 313).

Hjalti, a pawn of story, goes off to find the missing champion, finds him sitting idle in the king's hall, and with harsh reproaches calls on him to exert the power of those arms which were as strong as a bear's. Bjarki stands up, sighing. Hjalti, he says, has done the king an ill turn in thus disturbing him. Victory was close at hand, but now all must take its course as he gives the king such diminished aid as he can. He goes out to fight in human form, and the bear had already vanished away from their host. This menacing and almost victorious beast was Bjarki's *fylgja*, his fetch or animal familiar, the personification of his essential being, stronger and abler against other-world foes than any man or half-man. With his vanishing the tide of battle turned against them.

Queen Skuld, where she sat in her black tent on her witch's scaffold, had not brought any of her tricks into play while the bear was in king Hrolf's host; but there was now such a change as when dark night follows the bright day. King Hrolf's men could see where a monstrous boar advanced from king Hjorvarth's ranks. To look at he was not less than a three year ox in size and wolf-grey in colour, an arrow flew from each of his bristles, and in such sinister fashion he felled king Hrolf's liegemen in swathes (pp. 314–15).

This was a boar altogether more destructive of our human kind than the boar worshipped at Uppsala by king Athils, which got such a hiding from the hound Gram. In all probability it was Odinn, whom Bjarki in the *Bjarkamál* was content to call 'the awful husband of Frigg . . . mighty in battle, content ever with a single eye', but whom he here apostrophizes as 'Herjan's foul and faithless son. . . . Could anyone but point him out to me, I would squeeze him like any other vile and tiniest mousling. Wicked, poisonous beast, shameful would be his handling if I might lay hold of him!'

Bear and Boar might be thought enough, with the War-God's malice and the witchcraft of Skuld. But *Hrólfs Saga* uncovers a still more hideous corner of ancient belief and story. Hew as he may, till he is up to his shoulders in blood, Bjarki cannot see that the enemy host grows fewer. 'Endless is Skuld's host', he cries. 'I fear now that the dead stir here, rise up again and fight against us, and hard will it prove to fight with fetches; and for all so many limbs as here are cloven, shields split, and helms and corslets hewn in pieces, and many a chieftain cut asunder, these the dead are now the grimmest to contend with.' And later:

A while since I encountered king Hjorvarth in an earlier assault, so that we clashed head on, and neither of us flung insult at the other. We had a passage of arms for a time. He dispatched a blow at me whereby I scented death; I cut away his arm and leg. A further blow reached his shoulder, and thus I split him down through side and back, and he so altered mien at this that he did not so much as gasp, and it was as if he slept for a while. I thought him dead, and but few of his kind will be found, for he fought on no less dauntlessly than before, and I shall never be able to tell what gave him strength (p. 316).

These were *draugar*, the risen dead or living corpses who are a gruesome feature of Old Norse belief and charge with horror many a widespread saga and folktale. Interestingly enough, their absence from *Bjarkamál* increases that poem's heroic tension, by holding it on a superhuman not a supernatural level. Yet though the cloven king rose and fought again, the saga tells us in the end that he fell there in battle with all his host, save for a few skulkers who survived along with the abominable Skuld. On these vengeance was taken by Bjarki's brothers Elgfrothi and Thorir Houndsfoot, with a reinforcement from queen Yrsa in Sweden led by king Hrolf's name-fastener Vogg.

But in Saxo's prose sequel to the fall of Hrolf, Hiartuarus is very much alive, though only for a short time. That same day he held a victory-feast and with a victor's rhetoric marvelled at the loyalty and will to annihilation of Hrolf's followers. At this one survivor came forth, Hrolf's name-fastener Vogg, here named Viggo, and said he was willing to take service with Hiartuarus. The usurper proffered him a sword, point forward, but Viggo asked that it should be offered him hilt forward, as was Hrolf's practice when he gave a sword. The gratified Hiartuarus reversed hilt and point, but as soon as Viggo set hand to hilt he drove the point right through him, thus keeping his promise to avenge Hrolf Kraki on his slayer. 'Thus the royalty of Hiartuarus was won and ended on the same day.' *Skjöldunga Saga* tells the same tale of Hiorvardus and Woggerus, concluding: 'Thus Hiorvardus was the only man who has ruled the Danish kingdom for barely six hours.'

17. NEWS OF SKJOLD (SCYLD) AND THE SKJOLDUNGS
Saxo Grammaticus, Angers MS.

...pimenta fuere ut ab ipo ceti danoꝛ re

...s communi q̄dā uocabulo scoldungi nu

† b̄ q̄cu̅ uiꝰ stabi̅tent̅ a. m. p̄etereꞇ b̄ꝗ etaꞇ sta. clarissimiꞇ ind̄

...parentur. Precurrebat igitur sciold<us>   expimiꞇ. † animi uig̅

ecia fulgore suo finium

occupauit.

...r̄m complementu̅ animi maturitate

ocꞇla   † q̄ iuꝛ spectaꞇoꝛ ob renidinē ēē poterat

...flictus q̄; gessit quoꝛ eum uix specta

(b̄ spectatu̅ obtente̅ritate ēē poterat.

...em etas ēē paciebatur. Inquo annoꝛ uir   Ꝑ hic̅ arini

ecia pat̅ car

te q̄ spiciuꞇ fu̅

† p̄uentio   tiꞇ. Sid̄ impi

...tiꞇ q̄; p̄cursu̅ ob aliuldā saxonum regis fi   ges abrogant̅ ꞇ

tar̄ꞇ tulit ꞇ q̅

† gr̄a   b̄ p̄cabat   emdand̅ pate sh̄

...m quā summe pulc̄tudiniꞇ intuitu postu

ꝉ̄ earu̅dem nupciaꝛ.   art

illa ducꞇ   sim

...bat cum scato allemannie satrapa ei   dilig̅ria p̄sheiꞇ:

† itaq̅ regnu̅ pac

...m puelle competitore teutonu̅· danoꝛ   ꝓ bitate amissā

tuce recipauit. Ꝑ

...excercitu inspectante ex puocacione d̄i   recidenda̅ r̅ ma

lionu̅ legerculiꞇ

...ucauit interfecto q̄; eo omnem allemā   suu̅ qꝺ fuere libi

donauat clandeꞇ

insidiiꞇ petit. Ꝑo

...annoꝛ gentem p̄inde ac ducis sui in   n soliꞇ domeṡ̄ ꞇ ꞇ

diuꞇ colebat ꝓ ea

tiꞇ ex hoste ꞇ b̄iꞇ

† tbuto adegit.   mare solitꞇ † d̄

...rtu debellatam tributi lege choer̄   pecunia ad̄

† tbutaria pensioue idomuit.   g̅lam ad diuꞇ

...undare debē rē̄tat. Omniu̅ ꞇ alienūs ex fisco suo soluebat

...ca alioꝛ regu̅ foꞇitudine̅ munificencia ac libalitate certabat

...cerent. fomentiꞇ u̅sqꞇ remedia ꝗc maiurꞇ alĺheꞇ ꞇ b

3. Deaths and Stratagems

Some way back we said that the first business of the authors of the *Fornaldar Sögur*, the Sagas of Olden Times, was to entertain. And entertain they did. But no form of entertainment is the worse for a little art, and to pursue the metaphor, we should now give some attention not only to the nature of the act but to the quality of the performance. How good is *Hrólfs Saga* in terms of its story-telling? How well is it done? And in what fashion?

First, then, its construction. If we are naïve enough to think that a Saga of Olden Times which describes itself as *Hrólfs Saga Kraka* (this is the witness of the primary MSS) should confine itself after the fashion of yesterday's 'well-made novel' to the affairs of its named hero, and to those alone, without question we must conclude that it is badly constructed. Thus a quarter of the saga is past before we get any mention of Hrolf. 'He (Helgi) and Yrsa loved each other dearly and had a son who was called Hrolf and with the passing of the years became a man of great renown.' When he is next mentioned two-fifths of the saga are past, and he *is* a man of great renown. He takes Svipdag into his service, assesses the prospect of recovering his father's treasure from the Swedes, and tricks Hjorvarth into becoming his tributary-king. When he is next mentioned three-fifths of the saga are past, and Bothvar Bjarki has sought his court and service.[1]

[1] To put it another and more arithmetical way: the Editiones Arnamagnææ edition of *Hrólfs Saga Kraka* fills 124 pages (plus 2 lines). Hrolf gets his first mention, the sentence quoted above, on page 29, and plays no part in the saga before pages 46–51. He is next mentioned on page 70, and puts in a personal appearance on page 76. Thereafter the saga is at all times concerned with him and his champions.

18. A TAPESTRY FROM OSEBERG
Processional with figures on foot or mounted, men, women, horses, carts, weapons, birds, and formal symbols.

But granted the nature of a legendary saga, this is not as ill-planned as may appear. Like king Arthur and the emperor Charlemagne, king Hrolf would be lost without his champions. We have a roll-call of these when hostility bares its face at Lejre. 'Then up started Hromund the Hard and Hrolf the Quickhanded, Svipdag and Beigath and Hvitserk the Valiant, Haklang the sixth, Hardrefil the seventh, Haki the Brave the eighth, Vott the Powerful the ninth, Starolf (thus named) the tenth, Hjalti the Magnanimous the eleventh, and Bothvar Bjarki the twelfth.' It is unthinkable that a story-teller would narrate, or an audience accept, a saga about king Hrolf which did not offer expected because traditional information about some or all of these worthies. And sure enough the MSS which begin as the Saga of King Hrolf Kraki (*Hier byriar Söguna af Hrolfe Konge Kraka*, et var.) end as the Saga of King Hrolf Kraki and his Champions (*endar hier sögu Hrólfs kongs Kraka og kappa hans*). Therefore the saga's third 'story', about the brothers Svipdag, Beigath and Hvitserk, and how they became king Hrolf's champions, and the fourth 'story' about Bothvar Bjarki, and how he and Hjalti became king Hrolf's champions, must be held essential to the sagaman's design. Further the most celebrated feat of king Hrolf's life, as distinct from his death, was his expedition to king Athils's court at Uppsala, and the sagaman sees that necromantic ruffian as Hrolf's obverse at all times and in every respect. At Lejre all is honour and light, but 'king Athils is a grim man, and not trustworthy, though his outward showing is a fair one; while his men, though mighty, are full of malice. Yet admittedly king Athils is a powerful and famous man.' 'The Story of Svipdag' is also the story of king Athils, and on that count likewise relevant to the main theme. Which brings us to another important particular.

Before Svipdag seeks his court Athils is already inextricably entangled in king Hrolf's affairs. By his marriage to queen Yrsa he is Hrolf's step-father; he is also the slayer of Hrolf's father and purloiner of his treasure. The sagaman who did not tell us about all this would not be doing his job, and to tell us about this it was essential to tell us about earlier matters too. So we have the story of Helgi and how he had a wife who was also his daughter. And, as ever, one thing leads to another. Hrolf's half-sister Skuld who would be the main instrument of his downfall; his famous uncle Hroar and cousin Hraerek with whom his legendary connections were powerful if confusing in both Scandinavian and English tradition—we begin to see that from a contemporary point of view *Hrólfs Saga* has been under way not from page 58, not from page 46, not even from page 29, but by our Editiones count from page 16. This leaves the early Skjoldung material relating to Halfdan and his brother, and if one accepts the genealogist's principle that once you get back to Noah and the Ark you may as well get back to Adam, there is no impropriety about its inclusion. Two further generalities are relevant: the saga, despite its title, was meant to be about three generations of Skjoldungs; and we should not forget that *Skjöldunga Saga*, Saxo's *Danish History*, Snorri's *Skáldskaparmál*, and *Hrólfs Saga* itself suggest that the Hrolfian material required amplification if a saga and not a *þáttr* was to emerge.

In fact the saga consists of a series of reasonably well connected *þættir*, or short stories. With allowance for the difference of literary kinds developed with almost a millennium in between, we might describe its author's technique as a short story writer's, not a novelist's. First, he puts his saga together in six clearly defined sections relating to (1) Frothi and Halfdan, (2) Helgi and Hroar, (3) Svipdag (and Athils), (4) Bothvar Bjarki, (5) the Uppsala ride, and (6) the holocaust at Lejre. Second, and this is no less significant, he builds up his first five sections from wondertale and legendary motifs of the kind already discussed, anecdotes, antiquarian rumination, accepted types and stock responses, and other such lumber of the learned and literary mind. How much he rejected or stayed ignorant of we shall never know, but we can guess. He appears to have heard of Agnarus, who on the authority of Saxo and the *Bjarkarímur* relinquished his life with a smile, but appears content to replace him with a nameless berserk, while his own Agnarr, recklessly styled Hroar's son, is allowed the honour of recovering the Skjoldung's treasure-ring from the fjord into which the envious Hrok had flung it. He tells of Vogg's name-fastening, but not of Vogg's sword-thrusting vengeance. Yet on the whole he is generous in his use of good detail. The putting together of his sections involves him in a great many doublets. A sorceress on a high scaffold or platform plays a treacherous part when the boys Hroar and Helgi were first in Frothi's hall; a sorceress on her witch's scaffold in her black tent uses her magic against Hrolf at Lejre. A cruel stepmother changes the mother-to-be of Skuld into a repulsive fugitive, and a cruel stepmother changes the father of Bothvar into a bear. Bothvar is made to drink a strengthening draught of blood from Elgfrothi's elk-leg, Hott the same from the winged monster. There is a name-fastening for Hott and another for king Hrolf. Frothi has a dream warning and fateful, Svip a dream warning and helpful. The similarities between the appropriate parts of Svipdag's and Bothvar's stories have been touched on, more especially the response of each to the berserk's challenge. Thorir Houndsfoot had a backside the breadth of two men's backsides, by virtue of which he came to fill the throne of the Gauts; Bothvar required two men's seats to himself when he and Hott moved up in Hrolf's hall. We noticed this same occurrence of doublets in *Culhwch and Olwen* (see pp. 73 and 77). In *King Hrolf's Saga* they are invariably helpful to the story.

Our author is not unaware of the need for links between his story sections. Some of these maybe owe more to our imagination than his skill—like the echoed malice and hypocrisy of Frothi and Athils. Others we tend to overlook, like Svipdag's being granted the right to ask for the lives of twelve men at Athils's hand, and claiming that right when he leads Hrolf and the other eleven champions into Athils's hall. The motif makes no particular impression because it lacks the dramatic impact of an unwillingly granted boon, and serves only to re-establish the already well-established fact of Athils's incorrigible double-dealing. *Skjöldunga Saga* and Saxo end their tale of Hrolf when Vogg takes vengeance for him; but the author of *Hrólfs Saga* is even more concerned with the vengeance for Bothvar Bjarki, and this is carried out as had been promised him (see p. 150 above) by his brothers Elgfrothi and Thorir Houndsfoot. But the most effective of these linking and causative devices is Skuld. Like other heroes Hrolf was not born to win the last battle and live happily ever after. He was born to live gloriously, be defeated, and die gloriously. Skuld is his doom-note. Together with Odinn she will bring not only warriors but the powers of darkness against him. He cannot withstand almighty fate. 'No man outlives the evening, after the norns' decree.' But on the whole it may be admitted, the saga does not exceed the sum of its parts.

In other words, what remains in the reader's mind is less the effect of the whole saga than the impression made by this or that episode. If for the moment we leave aside our author's reworking of *Bjarkamál*, where we might argue that most of his work was done for him, we are probably most impressed by his version of Hrolf's expedition to Uppsala, and thereafter by the antics of Hott-Hjalti. The former is much the finer: it has a sufficiency of contrasted characters, the heroic and dignified Hrolf, the grotesque yet formidable Athils, the queenly Yrsa; a profusion of episode, often by way of snare and counterstroke, attack and counterblast; and not least, a darkening shroud of magic and evil. The impressionistic portrayal of the hall where much of the action takes place, its indeterminate size, the unstated nature of its dangerous floor, the undefined curtainings whose every fold hid an armed man, the unknown numbers of these men, the movable throne and hollow wooden pillar—'while so great a murk enshrouded king Athils that they could only vaguely distinguish his features'—add hosts and heroes, dog, boar, hawks and horses, the one-eyed wargod and the swine-bowing of him who was mightiest of the Swedes, and we have all the concomitants of a pre-gothic Gothic Tale, told with force, fervour, and precision. And we can add our own and private ironies to this famed encounter of monarchs in which Athils lost his bottom and Hrolf his good luck.

There is a note of high, savage comedy present through most of this adventure of which our author was surely aware. At any rate it is not found in Saxo's version of the events. When Saxo introduces the name-fastening episode connected with Viggo (Vogg) as 'a thing that it is mirthful to record', the very phrase is sedative to mirth. Save in the manner of his death,[1] there is nothing in Saxo,

---

[1] Athils, says Saxo, was cut off ignominiously. 'For whilst, in great jubilation of spirit, he was honouring the funeral rites of Rolf with a feast, he drank too greedily, and paid for his filthy intemperance by his sudden end' (III, 75). Snorri's *Ynglinga Saga* has a different tale to tell. 'King Athils was present at a sacrifice to the *dísir* (guardian spirits, goddesses), and rode his horse round the goddess's hall. The horse stumbled beneath him and fell, and the king was

any more than in *Skjöldunga Saga*, Snorri's *Skáldskaparmál* and *Heim-skringla*, to suggest that they or their sources were aware of the literary possibilities of Athils's person, character, and setting which *Hrólfs Saga* exploits so zestfully. In the Hott-Hjalti episodes there is the same zest, but a different kind of humour, rough, brutal, crude, and probably better suited to the homelier kind of listener. Even so the telling is not devoid of nice touches. When Hott's mother has told Bothvar about her son's plight, how the king's men have seized Hott and put him on their bone-heap to use as a target, she makes a request: 'I would have this return from you for my hospital-ity, that you throw smaller rather than bigger bones at him, if he is not by this time dead and gone.' Hott's bone-wall is a kitchen parody of the heroic shield-wall, and in true saga fashion we may read our own conclusions into the blackness of Hott's protruding hand and the circumstance that Bothvar, with the same sense of the immediately useful which made Robinson Crusoe begin his course of improvement by clapping a pair of drawers on Man Friday, carries him off to a nearby pond and washes him from top to toe. The bone that brought about Bothvar's intervention at the feast was a knuckle-bone—but with a neat sense of timing the narrator lets us know that it had the leg-bone attached. When Bothvar catches it in flight and hurls it back, we should be remembering that to pluck a hostile spear out of mid-air and hurl it back at the thrower was a feat attributed to heroes as celebrated as Culhwch of Wales and Gunnar of Lithend. And at all times during the 'Making of Hott' we must be clear that our fledgling modern unwillingness to be amused by the sight of human beings in a state of terror was felt even more rarely by narrators or audiences in saga times. Hott's shrieks and tremblings were intended to be funny and *were* funny. When in *Atlakviða*, and still more in *Atlamál in Grœnlenzko*, it is proposed to cut the living heart out of the thrall Hjalli, we are not invited to feel sympathy for him. He is in a panic, cries out, runs from corner to corner, wants to be left with his pigs, be given the dirtiest work, dung fields, anything so long as he may be left alive. Inevitably we *do* feel sympathy for him, and horror at the code of

thrown, and his head struck a stone so that the skull broke, and his brains were all over the stone.' *Hrólfs Saga* makes no report of his end.

conduct which forbids it. *Gwell ci byw na llew marw*: 'Better a live dog than a dead lion.' But these are unheroic thoughts.[1]

The device by which Hott receives credit for killing the winged monster in fact killed by Bothvar is clumsy in itself and in its telling. (The device incidentally is one of the reasons why it is difficult to identify closely this particular exploit of Bothvar Bjarki's with any one of Beowulf's exploits.) The king's courtiers are heroes but are also cowards; Bothvar has an unexplained difficulty with his sword Laufi; the dead beast is stationary but the watchmen report that it is rushing furiously towards the stronghold; king Hrolf (because he is to part with it, no doubt) is wearing the sword Gullinhjalti, not the sword Skofnung for ever associated with his name; and so splendid a king must not be deceived as to what is happening, though one judges that the original story required that he should be. But these too are unheroic thoughts, and doubtless we should cravenly conclude, as many times before, that a pattern of folktale motifs, interwoven and overlaid, leads to complications, and that these complications were not troublesome to their proper audience.

The draughts of blood which improved Hott's strength and valour did nothing for his understanding. At his best he never really rids himself of the cumbersome image of Strong John. His last dalliance with his mistress either shows heroic convention at its most humourless, which is possible, or deliberately parodies it, which is not unlikely, or simply and traditionally provides a hard-stomached audience with a hard-hearted folktale jest. As he went off to her embraces he observed that things were less than peaceful in the tents of Hjorvarth and Skuld. However he chose not to be perturbed, lay down with his girl, and when at last he sprang up, it was to ask her the extraordinary question: 'Which strikes you as the better, two at twenty-two or one at eighty?' Said she: 'Two at twenty-two strike me as better than old fellows of eighty.' For which sensible answer he went up close to her and bit off her nose. Our author, who may have misunderstood his source, lets this go

---

[1] The murder of archbishop Ælfeah by the Danish army in 1012 is a factual parallel to *Hrólfs Saga*'s Danish bone-throwing. 'They pelted him to death with bones and the heads of cattle . . .' His killers were drunk and no doubt merry (*Anglo-Saxon Chronicle*, E, *sub anno*).

without direct comment, but does allow the girl to say that she has
been ill used. The well-lettered Saxo avoids the first idiocy of
Hjalti's ignoring a hostile army, and mitigates the second by letting
Hjalti's mistress ask, as he went off to battle, how old a man he
thought she ought to marry if he didn't come back. For which
'wanton question' he invited her to come close and cut off her nose,
and by thus resorting to a traditional punishment for a faithless
woman earned Saxo's clerkly approbation. But as we have stated,
the *Fornaldar Sögur* are strong on horror, some of it ludicrous, most
of it crude, and *Hrólfs Saga* in this respect is not among the worst.

Crude, ludicrous, disgusting, however we view it, the incident
conducts us yet again to the saga's end and climax, the assault on
Lejre by fire and sword, and the death there of Hrolf and all his
champions. Our author's sources, and more especially what he knew
of the *Bjarkamál*, were compulsive for him; but we should not therefore diminish his credit for the tact and power with which he used
them. We have said that in *Bjarkamál* there is no bear, no boar, no
sorceress, no living dead, nor do Hjalti and Bjarki promise themselves life and feasting with their peers in Valhalla. The poem is not
cast in narrative form, but is a sequence of harangues, *exhortacionum
series*, in metrical shape, set in the mouths of the two heroes, in
which they exhort each other to do brave deeds, die gloriously, fall
dauntless with their lord. Like the Welsh *Gododdin*, *Bjarkamál* is
purely heroic.

'Sweet is it to repay the gifts received from our lord, to grip the
swords, and devote the steel to glory. . . . Let us do with brave
hearts all the things that in our cups we boasted with sodden
lips. . . . My master is the greatest of the Danes. . . . Nothing was
so fair to him that he would not lavish it, or so dear that he would not
give it to his friends, for he used treasure like ashes, and measured his
years by glory and not by gain. . . . Let our drawn swords measure
the weight of our service. Fame follows us in death, and glory shall
outlive our crumbling ashes! and that which perfect valour hath
achieved during its span shall not fade for ever and ever . . .

'War springs from the nobly born: famous pedigrees are the makers
of War. For the perilous deeds which chiefs attempt are not to be done
by the ventures of common men. . . . Already the hard edges and

the spear-points have cleft my shield in splinters, and the ravening steel has rent and devoured its portions bit by bit in the battle. . . .

'Let a noble death come to those that fall before the eyes of their king. While life lasts let us strive for the power to die honourably and to reap a noble end by our deeds. I will die overpowered near the head of my slain captain, and at his feet thou also shalt slip on thy face in death, so that whoso scans the piled corpses may see in what wise we rate the gold our lord gave us. We shall be the prey of ravens and a morsel for hungry eagles, and the ravening bird shall feast on the banquet of our body. Thus should fall princes dauntless in war, clasping their famous king in a common death.'[1]

This is heroic poetry with none but heroic trappings, its joys and exaltations, as Ragnarr Hairybreeks is reported to have said on a comparable occasion, quite different from those of kissing a young widow in the best seat at table. But the author of *Hrólfs Saga* has a somewhat different task in hand. Not only must he conclude his saga of king Hrolf and his champion Bothvar; he is still involved

---

[1] Two narrative and several 'kenning' verses survive of an Icelandic *Bjarkamál*, in *fornyrðislag* metre and, the narrative two, in a suitably heroic context. On the morning of the battle of Stiklarstadir, which was to prove fatal to King (later Saint) Olaf's life and hopes, the king was awake early and asked his poet Thormod Troublesome-Skald to recite them a poem. 'Thormod sat up and recited in a good loud voice, so that the whole army could hear. He recited the "Old Lay of Bjarki", whose beginning is this:

Day has arisen,	Har the Hardgripper,
Cock thrashes his feathers,	Hrolf the good Bowman,
Time now for toilers	Men of high lineage
To take to their tasks.	Who never will flee;
Awake and be watchful,	Not for wine do I wake you,
Loved friends, now and always,	And whispering with women,
All you best comrades	But rather I rouse you
Of Athils's train.	To rough battle-play.

The soldiers were then awake, and when the poem was concluded men thanked him for the poem, and were well pleased with it. They thought it right for the occasion and called the poem *Húskarlahvöt*, 'The Housecarls' Whetting'. The king thanked him for his entertainment. Then the king took a gold arm-ring whose worth was half a mark and gave it to Thormod. Thormod thanked the king for his gift and said, "We have a good king, but it is hard to tell now how long he will live. It is my prayer, sire, that you do not let us be parted one from the other, in life or death."' *Heimskringla, Óláfs Saga Helga*, 208.

with Bjarki the Bear's Son. On the whole in this last scene of his he combines heroic legend and folktale in an entirely effective way. We have seen Hrolf, merry and dauntless, sit as it were to his own funeral ale, heard Hjalti's calls to action and Bjarki's vaunts and declamations. We have watched the warring of a huge concourse of men and supernatural beings, the defence of the Bear, the assault of the Boar and the Risen Dead, and felt the desperation of Bjarki's threat against Odinn, his agony of mind for the lord he has sworn to protect. 'Shameful would be his [Odinn's] handling if I might lay hold of him! And none in this world but would store more hatred in his heart, if he saw his liege-lord so treated as we now see ours.'

'It is not easy,' said Hjalti, 'to bend what is fated, nor to withstand supernatural power.' And with that they ended their talk.

King Hrolf defended himself well and valiantly and with greater courage than any man has known the like of. They made at him hard, and a ring was thrown around him of the very pick of Hjorvarth's and Skuld's host. Skuld had now come to the battle, and eagerly whipped on that vile gang of hers to attack king Hrolf, for she could see that his champions were not all that close beside him. This was the thing that harassed Bothvar Bjarki greatly, that he might not be of help to his lord, and so with other of those champions, for they were now as ready to die with him as they had been to live with him when they were in the flower of their youth. The king's entire bodyguard had now fallen, so that no one of them survived, and most of the champions were mortally wounded. . . .

And now there came such a storm of enchantment that the champions began to fall one across the other, and king Hrolf came out from the shield-wall and was as a man dead of exhaustion. There is no need to make a long tale of it: there fell king Hrolf and all his champions, gloriously (pp. 317–8).

By every convention of saga great men must be greatly avenged, and so it was with Hrolf. The annihilation at Lejre was matched by the annihilation of Skuld and all her brood.

Likewise, men who die gloriously must be gloriously laid in howe. Here, unexpectedly, our author reaches for true simplicity, and finds it.

19. SPLENDOUR OF GOLD, 2: NORWEGIAN SCABBARD-
MOUNTS OF THE SIXTH CENTURY

A burial mound was erected for king Hrolf, and his sword Skofnung laid beside him; and for each of his champions his mound, and some weapon beside him. And there ends the Saga of king Hrolf and his Champions (p. 318).

His Saga, but not his story. Breaking into a mound for treasure was an exploit attributed to many an early settler in Iceland, or sometimes to his father or son. One such son was Skeggi from Midfjord (Midfjarthar-Skeggi), whose father Skinna-Bjorn, Bjorn of the Furs, had been a trader into Russia. Skeggi was an adaptable kind of man, sailor, pirate, merchant, as occasion offered. Towards the end of the ninth century

he was plundering in the Baltic, and put in by Zealand in Denmark. He was picked on to break into the burial mound of king Hrolf Kraki, and took out of it Hrolf's sword Skofnung, and Hjalti's axe, and many other treasures; but he could not get hold of Laufi, for Bothvar was going to attack him, only king Hrolf defended him. Later he returned to Iceland and lived at Reykjar in Midfjord (*Landnámabók*, c. 140).

He brought the Gleamer (*skafa*, to scrape, rub clean, or polish) with him, but the Leaf (*laufi*) stayed with its strong-armed owner Bothvar. We hear of Skofnung several times thereafter, in several sagas. It was misused by the poet Kormak in a duel, (*Kormáks Saga*, 9 and 10), and borrowed but not brandished by Thorkel Eyjolfsson when he was brought to compound his quarrel with the outlaw Grim on Tvidægra heath (*Laxdæla Saga*, 57 and 58). Thorkel still had it with him when he was shipwrecked with a cargo of timber in Breida-fjord; it came ashore jammed into the boat's hull, and thereafter was worn by Thorkel's son Gellir. In his old age Gellir went on a pilgrimage to Rome and returned by way of Denmark, where he fell ill and received the last rites. 'After that he died and his body rests in Roskilde. Gellir had taken Skofnung with him, and it was never recovered: it had been taken from the burial mound of Hrolf Kraki' (*Laxdæla Saga*, 78). Gamle Lejre will be found today barely five miles west-south-west of the cathedral city of Roskilde, near the head of the fjord which bears the city's name, so it would be

20. SPLENDOUR OF WAR: NORWEGIAN VIKING SWORDS

pleasant to believe that by the restoring hand of providence Skofnung was returned to whence it had come.[1] But the nature of saga
tradition, and the circumstance that no trace of Hrolf's sixth-
century court can be found within the purlieus of Lejre, make it
likelier that Skofnung, whether it rings aloud in the skull of a foe
('For it was the nature of Skofnung that it sang aloud when it felt
the bone'), sighs in the flesh of Athils's buttocks, or is laid up
Valhalla-wards in a howe with its royal master, came from the
hand of a wordsmith not swordsmith, and belongs like so much else
in *King Hrolf's Saga*, *Culhwch and Olwen*, and *Beowulf*, not with History,
daughter of Truth, but with Poetry, the mother of Invention.

[1] See for an account of Skofnung and its saga appearances, H. R. Ellis Davidson, *The Sword in Anglo-Saxon England*, 1962, pp. 172–7.

Select Bibliography

1. Beowulf

Editions: by Fr. Klaeber, 3rd ed, Boston, 1950; by C. L. Wrenn, 2nd ed, London, 1961; by E. V. K. Dobbie, New York, 1953, repr. London and New York, 1965.

A. Bonjour, *The Digressions in Beowulf*, Oxford, 1950.

A. G. Brodeur, *The Art of Beowulf*, California, 1959.

Nora K. Chadwick, 'The Monsters and Beowulf', in *The Anglo-Saxons. Studies in some Aspects of their History and Culture presented to Bruce Dickins*, ed. Peter Clemoes, London, 1959.

R. W. Chambers, *Beowulf, an Introduction to the Study of the Poem*, with a Supplement by C. L. Wrenn, Cambridge, 1963.

R. Girvan, *Beowulf and the Seventh Century*, London, 1935.

W. W. Lawrence, *Beowulf and Epic Tradition*, Cambridge, Mass., re-issued 1961.

J. A. Leake, *The Geats of Beowulf*, Wisconsin, 1967.

F. Panzer, *Studien zur germanischen Sagengeschichte. I. Beowulf*, München, 1910.

K. Sisam, *The Structure of Beowulf*, Oxford, 1965.

G. V. Smithers, *The Making of Beowulf*, Durham, 1961.

J. R. R. Tolkien, 'Beowulf: The Monsters and the Critics', in *Proceedings of the British Academy*, 1936.

D. Whitelock, *The Audience of Beowulf*, Oxford, 1951.

2. Culhwch ac Olwen

There is no modern edition (indeed no edition at all) of *Culhwch ac Olwen*, presenting a text, introduction, notes, and glossary, and one must still use the diplomatic editions of *The Text of the Mabinogion and other Welsh Tales from the Red Book of Hergest* (John Rhys and J. Gwenogvryn Evans, Oxford, 1887) and *The White Book Mabinogion*

(J. Gwenogvryn Evans, Pwllheli, 1907). There is an edition in preparation by Professor Idris Ll. Foster.

W. J. Gruffydd, 'The Mabinogion', in *Transactions of the Honourable Society of Cymmrodorion*, 1912–13.

W. J. Gruffydd, *Math vab Mathonwy*, Cardiff, 1928.

W. J. Gruffydd, 'Mabon vab Modron', in *Y Cymmrodor*, XLII, 1931.

Kenneth H. Jackson, *The International Popular Tale and Early Welsh Tradition*, Cardiff, 1961.

A. O. H. Jarman, 'Y Mabinogi: Rhagarweiniad', in *Y Traddodiad Rhyddiaith*, II, Llandysul, 1972.

Gwyn Jones and Thomas Jones, *The Mabinogion* (the Golden Cockerel Mabinogion, 1948), Everyman's Library, 1949.

Thomas Jones, 'The Black Book of Carmarthen "Stanzas of the Graves"', Sir John Rhŷs Memorial Lecture, British Academy, 1967.

R. S. Loomis, *Wales and the Arthurian Legend*, Cardiff, 1956.

R. S. Loomis (ed.), *Arthurian Literature in the Middle Ages*, Oxford, 1959.

3. *Hrólfs Saga Kraka*

Editions: by Finnur Jónsson, Copenhagen, 1904; by D. Slay, Copenhagen, 1960 (see too the same editor's *The Manuscripts of Hrólfs Saga Kraka*, Copenhagen, 1960). Translation by Gwyn Jones in *Eirik the Red and other Icelandic Sagas*, pp. 219–318, World's Classics edition, London, 1966.

Jakob Benediktsson, *Arngrimi Jonæ opera latine conscripta*, in Bibliotheca Arnamagnæana, IX–XII (text of *Skjöldunga Saga* in IX), Copenhagen, 1950–7. Also 'Icelandic Traditions of the Scyldings', in *Saga-Book*, XV, 1957–9.

Hans Brix, *Analyser og Problemer: Undersøgelser i den ældre danske Litteratur*, II, Copenhagen, 1935.

Jón Helgason, 'Bjarkamál Saxa', in *Afmæliskveðju til Ragnars Jónssonar*, Reykjavík, 1954.

Paul Herrmann, *Erläuterungen zu den ersten neun Büchern . . . des Saxo Grammaticus*, Leipzig, 1922.

Axel Olrik, *Danmarks Heltedigtning. I, Rolf Krake og den ældre Skjoldungrække; II, Starkad den gamle og den yngre Skjoldungrække*, Copenhagen, 1903–10. English translation and revision, L. M. Hollander, *The Heroic Legends of Denmark*, New York, 1919.)

4. *Miscellaneous*

Antti Aarne and Stith Thompson, *The Types of the Folktale, A Classifica-*

tion and Bibliography, 2nd revision, Academia Scientiarum Fennica, Helsinki, 1961.

Inger M. Boberg, *Motif-Index of Early Icelandic Literature*, Bibliotheca Arnamagnaeana XXVII, Copenhagen, 1966.

G. N. Garmonsway, Jacqueline Simpson, Hilda Ellis Davidson, *Beowulf and its Analogues*, London, 1968.

M. Cl. Gertz, *Scriptores Minores Historiae Danicae Medii Ævi*, I–II, Copenhagen, 1917–22, re-issue of 1970.

Kenneth H. Jackson, *The Gododdin*, Edinburgh, 1969.

A. O. H. Jarman, 'The heroic ideal in early Welsh poetry', in *Beiträge zur Indogermanistik und Keltologie: Julius Pokorny zum 80. Geburtstag gewidmet*, herausgegeben von W. Heid, Innsbruck, 1967.

Gwyn Jones, *A History of the Vikings*, London, 1968.

The Battle of Maldon, ed. E. V. Gordon, London, 1937.

Hermann Pálsson and Paul Edwards, *Legendary Fiction in Medieval Iceland*, Studia Islandica 30, Reykjavík, 1971.

Saxo Grammaticus: *Saxonis Gesta Danorum*, ed. A. Holder, Strassburg, 1886; J. Olrik and H. Raeder, Copenhagen, 1931, with Index Verborum ed. Franz Blatt, 1936 and 1938. Translation by Oliver Elton, *The First Nine Books of the Danish History of Saxo Grammaticus*, 1894 (based on Holder).

Stith Thompson, *Motif-Index of Folk-Literature*, 6 vols, 2nd edition, Copenhagen, 1955–8.

C. Weibull, *Källkritik och historia*, Stockholm, 1964.

L. Weibull, *Nordisk Historia*, ed. Sture Bolin and others, Stockholm, 1948.

Sir Ifor Williams, *Canu Aneirin*, Cardiff, 1938.

Index

I: Index of Proper Names

II: Brief Index of the More Important Beast and Story References

Photograph by Julian Sheppard for the Welsh Arts Council

GWYN JONES is Professor of English Language and Literature at the University College, Cardiff, and earlier held the Chair of English at the University College of Wales, Aberystwyth. He was for eleven years a member of the Arts Council of Great Britain and Chairman of the Welsh Arts Council; and is a Past President of the Viking Society for Northern Research. In 1963 the President of Iceland conferred on him the decoration of Knight of the Order of the Falcon; and in 1964 he was made a Commander of the Order of the British Empire.

þ edeſul leodum þreaum iſ...
feond heoꝼa dypl aneſ cꝛaꝼt ealle
oꝼeꝛ comon ſel þeꝛ mihtum god iſ ge aꝛ
ꝛed þ mihtɀg god manna cynneſ peol
feꝛhð com on þanþe niht ſcyþdan
du ɀenɀa ſceoꝛend ſpꝛæron þa þ hoꝼa
þeced heal dan ſceoldon ealle buton an
þ þæſ yldum cuþ þ hie ne moſte þanne
nolde ſe ſyn ſcaþa undeꝛ ſceadu þꝛeꝛ
dan þac he þæccende ꝼꝛaþum oꝛandan
bad bolɀen mod beadþa ɀe þinɀeſ

Da com of moꝛe undeꝛ miſt hleoþum ɠꝛen
del ɠonɠan godeſ yꝛꝛe bæꝛ myꝛceꝛ
ſe man ſcaða manna cynneſ ſumne b
ſyþþan in ſeleɀ þam hean þod undeꝛ
num to þæſ þe he þin þeced ɠold ſele ɠum
na ɠeapþoſt þiſſe þæt ɀum þaþne ne
þæſ þæt ꝼoꝛma ſið þ he hꝛoþ ɠaꝛeſ hu
 ɀeſohte næꝼꝛe he on aldoꝛ daɀum diꝛe